STUDIES IN FRENCH LITERATU

Gene

W. C

MOLIÈRE: TARTUFFE

by

H. GASTON HALL

Reader in French, University of Warwick

EDWARD ARNOLD

First published 1960 by
Edward Arnold (Publishers) Ltd.
41 Bedford Square, London WC1B 3DQ

Reprinted 1963, 1965, 1970
Reprinted with amended bibliography 1976
Reprinted 1977, 1979, 1981

ISBN 0 7131 5508 6

Printed and bound in Great Britain at
The Camelot Press Ltd, Southampton

Contents

PAGE

1. BACKGROUND 7
   - The true and false 'dévot' 7
   - Milieu and Moment 8
   - Comic Realism 14
   - Comic Art 17
   - Comic Subject 19
   - Sources 23
   - Intentions 25
   - Changes 27

2. STRUCTURE 30
   - Act I 30
   - Act II 37
   - Act III 40
   - Act IV 45
   - Act V 48

3. STYLE 51

SELECT BIBLIOGRAPHY 63

1. *Background*

To enjoy *Tartuffe* it is important to know that to Molière's contemporaries every aspect of religion was an absorbing topic, but that one did not write about it in a comedy. This suggests why religious hypocrisy might have appealed to an ambitious rascal in 1664 and further suggests something of the impact of this comedy on early audiences. For to the first spectators, when a *Tartuffe* in three acts was performed at Versailles as part of the royal 'Plaisirs de l'île enchantée', it was not a 'classic' to be studied, but entertainment so boldly original that a powerful clique of the devout succeeded in banning it for five years despite the known favour of the King. Nor was it for observance of any 'rules' of playwriting that when the ban was lifted in February 1669 *Tartuffe* drew record crowds until the Lenten closing, despite an interdict by the Archbishop of Paris. To the subjects of Louis XIV, at loggerheads on the nature of Christianity, both content and presentation of *Tartuffe* were extraordinarily relevant.

The true and false 'dévot'

To us the strategy of Molière's impostor may seem improbable. But before dismissing it as unrealistic, one should realize that Paris teemed with men of all rank who affected piety. 'Since the beginning of the century', writes the author of the best history of seventeenth-century French literature, 'the "dévot" had become a social type, like the monk or the hermit of the Middle Ages.'[1] What may be called the 'lay director' was especially common. Such men, who often had ill-defined if any ties with the established ecclesiastical order, entered families,

[1] Antoine Adam, *Histoire de la littérature française au XVIIe siècle*, Paris, 1956, III, 298.

heard confessions, directed prayers and in many matters of conscience behaved like professional clergy. A number of them rose to positions of considerable influence.

Devoutness was a way to power. It is hardly surprising then that unscrupulous men sought power by feigning it. 'Le nom de la vertu sert à l'intérêt aussi utilement que les vices', remarks La Rochefoucauld. If we believe another contemporary, La Bruyère, the 'faux dévot' was also a familiar social type. One such man, Charpy de Sainte-Croix, a forger and the author of an unsanctioned mystical treatise, had recently seduced the wife of one of Molière's neighbours after receiving shelter in the household. It is often suggested that Molière had Charpy in mind when he wrote *Tartuffe*. But there were others. In 1667 the Italian actor Bendinelli, who played leading rôles under the name Valère, was betrayed by a priest staying in his home in much the same way that Tartuffe betrays Orgon. It may be that Molière had this incident in mind when he revised his play for the single performance he gave of a bowdlerized *Imposteur* four months later. The coincidence in any case is striking evidence of what has always been called Molière's 'realism'. The more we learn of the seventeenth-century religious background, the less improbable Tartuffe's behaviour seems. It fits into a pattern of society and belief radically different from ours.

Milieu and Moment

For between *Tartuffe* and us lies like a great divide one of the really significant historical changes in basic attitudes, deeper in many ways than that which divides the Renaissance from the Middle Ages. It involves what a distinguished French scholar calls the 'crisis of the European conscience'. To view *Tartuffe* in something of its original proportions therefore requires no little effort of the imagination. That this comedy almost certainly contributed to these changes of attitude makes the effort worthwhile. The play is still relevant today.

Tartuffe is remarkable for containing within its own framework most of the information we require. A good performance brings much of this into proper focus so that scant commentary is required. In particular it shows that comic situations, rather than ideas, abstract study of character, or even satire, were the principal concern of the author, who was also the first producer-director and creator of what many feel to be the leading rôle, Orgon. The comic value of rhythm and gesture in *Tartuffe* will be discussed. But first a few more historical remarks should make it easier to savour the comedy of its verse and gesture alike.

To begin with, it is probably helpful to recall that in a city lacking modern newspapers, not to say radio and television, it is hardly an exaggeration to say that devotional tracts and doctrinal disputes were read in the 1660's by many people very much as the sports page or the stock market report is read today. Also the public for such reading had been greatly broadened (though we must not imagine it broad in the modern sense) by publication a few years earlier of Pascal's *Lettres provinciales*, to which there are distinct references in *Tartuffe*. The *Provinciales* are noteworthy also for comic treatment of the religious crisis which affected so many people in France.

Under the personal rule of Louis XIV, moreover, political discussion was treasonable unless favourable; there is none in this play. *Tartuffe* contains a few of the rare political allusions in all Molière, and these are discreet (*cf.* 181) or flattering (the Exempt); and not even the Exempt (a police officer) corresponds to contemporary legal practice. Economic and social first principles are never called into question. Manners are attacked; the basic structure of society is not. It would be as anachronistic to look for this in *Tartuffe* as for penicillin or helicopters. The very freedom with which Dorine speaks to her master in his own interest puts her loyalty beyond question and points up the difference between *Tartuffe* and the political comedies of the eighteenth century, not to say the 'angry young men' of the theatre today. When she opposes Orgon's plan to marry Mariane to Tartuffe, the argument is never that a grown daughter should have the right to choose her own husband. It is that a wise father must consider his daughter's personality in making his choice for her. Dorine exhorts Mariane to find a way to change or delay her father's plan; she never suggests that a father's authority should be less because he might be stupid and selfish. There is comedy rather than social reform in the fact that the servant in this scene is obviously right and the master wrong, precisely because it overturns an unchallenged 'natural' order.

This is clearer perhaps in the way we are shown Tartuffe himself. His ambitious scheme is patently grotesque, seen mainly in the externals of hypocrisy. If ever we glimpse the inner bundle of desires which impel him, humanly, to advance his interests through deceit, it is only in comic juxtaposition with the mask of his pose, as in the attempted seduction of Elmire: 'Ah! pour être dévot, je n'en suis pas moins homme' (966). Allusions to his original poverty are those of scorn rather than sympathy (63, 484). If life in Tartuffe's 'petite ville' is predicted as catastrophic for all the dreams of Mariane (657), we are never shown with Tartuffe's own eyes the dreariness of the provincial life which he seeks to escape. Thibaudet has compared him in this respect with Julien Sorel, the hero of Stendhal's *Le Rouge et le Noir*. Julien is certainly no less hypocritical (he models his conduct partly on the rôle of Tartuffe, which he knows by heart), yet for most readers intensely sympathetic because events are treated more nearly from his point of view. Julien like Tartuffe is calculating, and like Tartuffe an unforeseen passion upsets him. The difference is that in Stendhal's novel we see Julien's hypocrisy grow out of an hypocritical society, whereas it is Tartuffe who reduces the 'sympathetic characters' to hypocrisy (*cf.* 1551). Nowhere in *Tartuffe* do we find the notion that a man of energy and imagination deserves to rise.

Religion on the other hand occupied a far more central position then than now. Great houses had chapels, and many influential men daily visited a church (like Orgon when he met Tartuffe) without its being thought at all unusual. Religion was a very serious matter. How serious may be gathered from the intensity of feelings which in this country a few years before had led to civil war, the closing of the theatres and puritan immigration to America. Social historians point out that many other factors were involved, but this does not alter the fact that religious feelings ran high. When *Tartuffe* was first performed France also had had religious civil war within living memory, and the party which eventually brought about the expulsion of the Huguenots by Revocation of the Edict of Nantes in 1685 already argued that war was threatening again. Even within French Catholic opinion a bitter quarrel raged between Jesuits and the stricter Jansenists whom Pascal had defended in the *Provinciales*. Its crisis coincided almost exactly with the period in which *Tartuffe* was banned, and a very real spiritual interest was felt to be at stake. One may recall that it led the young Jean Racine, whose second tragedy was performed by Molière's troupe the year after *Tartuffe*, to break with his Jansenist tutors at Port-Royal because they condemned the theatre. Neither Jesuits nor Jansenists especially welcomed *Tartuffe*, though principals on either side were pleased to find details which they considered satirical of the other. That Tartuffe speaks of rectifying 'le mal de l'action | Avec la pureté de notre intention' (1491–2) undoubtedly touches upon the Jesuit 'direction of intention' attacked in the seventh *Provinciale*.

An important current of *libertin* or free-thinking opinion should also be mentioned. In many cases it involved licence of manners, but the underlying intellectual position was of greater consequence. Through individuals like La Mothe Le Vayer, a friend of Molière's who was tutor to the Dauphin, the scepticism which characterized one aspect of the Renaissance was continued in seventeenth-century France. It has been asserted that Molière himself was a *libertin*, even an atheist. But no text of Molière's confirms this assertion, though many (including *Tartuffe* and its preface) contradict it. Suspicion nevertheless attaches to the fact that among Latin poets Molière translated Lucretius, a materialist.

His association with known *libertins* like La Mothe Le Vayer also suggests that his zeal was less than moderate, as indeed one might deduce from his having made acting his career at a time when actors were under a general ban of the Church. Also it was probably the *libertins*, or those with leanings toward free thought, who were the most delighted with *Tartuffe*, less for its expressed religious views than for its assumptions, its air of sanity and moderation, its clarity, and the joyful appeal to the evidence of one's eyes. Sorbière, a contemporary physician and admirer of Pierre Gassendi, the Epicurean, acclaimed *Tartuffe* the great masterpiece of comedy and bade Terence and Plautus, Aristophanes, Menander, and all modern writers to kneel before it in awe. Later, for Voltaire, *Tartuffe* seemed a forerunner of the Enlightenment; and opposing 'la vertu vraie et éclairée' of Cléante to the 'dévotion imbécile' of Orgon, he found the former's speeches 'le plus fort et le plus élégant sermon que nous ayons en notre langue'. *Tartuffe* voiced a new ethics. Another said of it: 'Si je me sauve, je lui devrai mon salut.'

But *Tartuffe* is not a *libertin* play. Everywhere Molière stresses that whatever satirical attack his work contains is directed, not against piety as such, but against the 'faux dévots', the 'counterfeiters' of piety whom he attacks alike in his first *Placet au Roi* in 1664 and again in the preface to the original edition in 1669. Much of the elaborate distinction which Cléante makes between mask and face, artifice and sincerity, appearance and truth, appears to have been added after August 1667, in order to leave no doubt as to the character of Tartuffe and of the satire intended. It can have escaped few, however, that the piety championed by Cléante is more restrained, more compromising, above all more rational and human than that on which Orgon insists.

Probably the most important thing about the background of *Tartuffe* is just this. *Libertins* and hypocrites aside, opinion was divided upon the very nature of the Christian life. Which activities are obligatory, and which damaging for salvation? Of those permitted, which the best? A devout party, represented in this play by Madame Pernelle and Orgon, condemned such worldly pleasures as casual visits, attractive clothes, and naturally the theatre itself:

> Ces visites, ces bals, ces conversations
> Sont du malin esprit toutes inventions

remarks Madame Pernelle (151–2). To others, however, as to most of the characters of *Tartuffe*, such activities seemed innocent enough and perfectly compatible with Christian ethics. Most (but not all) modern readers agree, yet they might not if the other party had prevailed. It is sobering to reflect that toward the end of his life in 1662 Blaise Pascal, to whom the scientific method is as much indebted as French comic style, is said to have nourished himself deliberately without tasting his food (singular sacrifice for a Frenchman). Beneath his hairshirt he seems to have worn an iron belt with spikes pointed inward. Whenever he felt he had sinned through pride, he struck it with his elbow to drive the points into his flesh.

Pascal was a true 'dévot'; and since there were many similarly devout, his experience suggests something of the atmosphere which Orgon would have thrust upon his family. It is inhuman. In speaking to his brother about Tartuffe, Orgon in fact says:

> Il m'enseigne à n'avoir affection pour rien,
> De toutes amitiés il détache mon âme;
> Et je verrais mourir frère, enfants, mère et femme,
> Que je m'en soucierais autant que de cela (276–9),

whereupon he flicks his thumbnail on his upper teeth. This invites Cléante's ironic rejoinder: 'Les sentiments humains, mon frère, que voilà!' (280). Cléante points up the comic ambivalence of Orgon's words, but the very choice of his words shows that Orgon's sentiments are being judged in human rather than transcendental terms. These lines involve two questions. The first is that Orgon misunderstands the Christian tradition by which God's creatures are only to be loved as an expression of their Creator (*cf.* 929–44). Tartuffe has led Orgon to use this concept of love as a pretext for despising his family. His lines parody (Molière makes him parody) an attitude on the duty of Christian love, as expressed by Néarque in *Polyeucte* (1643):

> Comme rien n'est égal à sa grandeur suprême,
> Il faut ne rien aimer qu'après lui, qu'en lui-même,
> Négliger, pour lui plaire, et femme, et biens, et rang (73–5).

But more important than Orgon's travesty of this attitude is the fact that, however sincere, the kind of piety affected by Orgon *must* in a sense be inhuman, because the ways of God take precedence over the ways of man. Also it is because *Tartuffe* seemed to humanize piety that members of the Compagnie du Saint-Sacrement wanted it suppressed. For if Molière makes it clear that he does not deny the value of piety as a way of life, he denies by implication its exclusive, indeed its primary claims. He questions whether it is the best way. With Cléante he admires instead those whose 'dévotion est humaine, est traitable' (390). Everything is in the word 'traitable', the background of which is relativist. 'Les exercices de la piété souffrent des intervalles . . .,' writes Molière in his preface to *Tartuffe*. To those committed by belief in absolutes to perpetual abnegation he replies: 'Je doute qu'une si grande perfection soit dans les forces de la nature humaine. . . .'

Comic Realism

The rôle chosen by Tartuffe as a way to power thus seems plausible enough. Like Charpy, he counterfeits a valuable coin. This does not mean of course that Tartuffe is a portrait of Charpy. Still less does it mean that Tartuffe represents a typical hypocrite or 'faux dévot' as such. Even in the seventeenth century La Bruyère noticed how badly Tartuffe plays this rôle, how far from the real thing lies the theatrical image. Obviously this hearty eater, this robust seducer, 'Gros et gras, le teint frais, et la bouche vermeille' (234), is quite unfitted to play the part of the saintly ascetic. No rascal with the slightest talent for hypocrisy would have dared sit down to dine upon '. . . deux perdrix, / Avec une moitié de gigot en hachis' (239–40). It may be argued that remarks on his diet by Dorine are suspect as coming from an enemy. But they are confirmed by the author's formal declaration in the preface: 'He does not hold the spectator in doubt a moment; he is recognized at once by the marks that I give him . . .' They are confirmed likewise by what we know of Du Croisy, the actor who created the rôle: he seems to have been rather fat.

Nor, reflects La Bruyère, should a really competent hypocrite ever boast like Tartuffe when he first appears on stage: 'Laurent, serrez ma haire avec ma discipline' (853), but instead allow it to be tacitly assumed that he wore a hairshirt and that he scourged himself in private. It must be lines of this nature that Molière had in mind as he continued the prefatory remarks quoted earlier: '. . . from one end to the other he says no word, he makes no gesture which does not depict for the spectators the character of a wicked man, and illuminate that of the truly good man I place opposite him.' Also that 'véritable homme de bien', Cléante, anticipates the objection of La Bruyère in the text of *Tartuffe* itself:

> Les bons et vrais dévots, qu'on doit suivre à la trace,
> Ne sont pas ceux aussi qui font tant de grimace (329–30).

Not only does Tartuffe lack naturally any disposition for piety, but he also overcompensates when he feigns it. He is so bad at pretending, observes a German scholar, that he can deceive only those who, like Orgon and Madame Pernelle, for some reason want to be deceived. 'Everywhere the ass looks out from under the lion's skin.'[1] In an image nearer Molière, the face of the rogue keeps popping from beneath the mask of the saint. Clearly Tartuffe is not a typical, but a comic, 'faux dévot'. The type is serious: this individual who deviates is comic. However sinister Tartuffe may appear in the later scenes, there is always a comic discrepancy between the man and his mask.

[1] Erich Auerbach, 'The Faux Dévot', in *Mimesis*, trs. W. Trask, New York: Anchor Books, 1957, p. 317.

A single line will illustrate this point. When Tartuffe sees Dorine for the first time, he offers her his handkerchief, saying: 'Couvrez ce sein que je ne saurais voir' (860). This is the 'mask of a pious attitude'.[1] But it should be imagined, as it is often played, preceded by a tell-tale gesture: Tartuffe with his eyes on stalks and his neck craned toward Dorine's bosom. It is true that a realistic hypocrite needs more self-control. But the contradiction here between man and mask is no accident. It is an important part of Molière's dramatic subject. His hypocrite is comic rather than strictly realistic.

Or rather this is realism of a different sort. On the one hand Tartuffe is altogether concrete and particular: 'Il a l'oreille rouge et le teint bien fleuri' (647). Within the limits allowed by contemporary portrayal by types, Molière fixes upon the specific, the individually real; and this represents an aspect of reality far more accurately than the general, typifying, verisimilar portraits which often pass for realism in literature. Indeed Molière's chief interest in this respect seems to lie in the ridiculous deviation of his individual personage from the customary and normal. In this sense Tartuffe's appearance, the outer man, is realistic. We have already seen that his ambitious scheme, which we may call the inner man, likewise was realistic enough. But neither descriptive nor historic realism is the important thing about the portrait of Tartuffe. The genius of Molière lies rather in the contradictions between two equally convincing portraits. This is not so much a departure from realism as realism of a different sort, a comic realism. Molière presents a man in contradiction with himself, the scheming 'inner man' posing as what so obviously he is not: calculated discrepancy between ascetic mask and greedy face, the unreckoned one between calculation and instinct. Scenes like those in which Tartuffe turns from Dorine, or touches Elmire's knee, thus deal with a very real comic phenomenon: conflicting intentions. This is the (essentially ethical) reality which primarily interests Molière. He transposes it into scenes

[1] W. G. Moore, *Molière, A New Criticism*, Oxford, 1949, p. 45.

or images of greater value than the sum of their descriptive parts precisely because those parts are contradictory. We may exclaim with Sainte-Beuve: 'Quelle vérité, et quelle invraisemblance!'

Comic Art

This goes some distance toward understanding Molière's comic art. But if Tartuffe is a comic character, it may be asked, why then is he not always funny? Thus posed, the question is not an easy one to answer. Indeed scholars (Michaut, Brunetière) have either denied that Tartuffe is comic at all or admitted it only grudgingly. But by 'comic' we do not necessarily mean the humorous or funny, although of course we do not mean to exclude it. Comedy deals with contradictions, departure from certain standards which (rightly or wrongly) are accepted as reasonable and sociable; and as we have seen Molière makes it deal with 'contrariétés' which had not been considered comic before, as ascetic and glutton in the same person. The incompatible elements are often easy to see, as when Dorine asks her infuriated master: 'Ah! vous êtes dévot, et vous vous emportez?' (552). We all understand that the man who lays a special claim to piety has no business to get angry. Anger is a deadly sin, and in this play Orgon has just praised Tartuffe's remorse 'D'avoir pris une puce en faisant sa prière, | Et de l'avoir tuée avec trop de colère' (309–10). Nor is it difficult to see that Tartuffe's scruples about this flea (which incidentally reflect an authentic tradition of piety, not to mention contemporary hygienic conditions) are ludicrous in terms of his behaviour toward Mariane, Damis, and of course Elmire.

But sometimes it is more difficult to appreciate the norm from which events are seen. As suggested earlier, significant changes have taken place in our view of things. Incongruities exist on many planes: social, moral, political and religious. The various norms from which they are observed do not all appear to have had the same value in the 1660's as they have today. If anything, the controversial judgements on *Tartuffe* suggest that even today the norms for different readers vary widely. Great care must be exercised lest we substitute our own norms for those of the author, or, as some say, the audience for which he wrote: 'la Cour et la Ville', the aristocratic following of the Court at Versailles before whom the play was first performed, together with the upper *bourgeoisie* of Paris for whom it was revived at the Palais-Royal, and a glimpse of which we are offered in this play.

It is well to remember that for these people laughter was often harsh, cruel or scandalous. The philosopher Bergson, in his celebrated book on *Laughter*, observes that our attitude in laughing is one of 'insensibilité' or dissociation of our feelings from the plight of the confused or unfortunate. Derisive laughter has been recorded at public executions. It is clear that certain events, however unhappy for the victims, are comic when viewed with detachment.

So it is with the theatre. 'We participate in a tragedy; at a comedy we only look.' Huxley expresses what many have thought. The mood of comedy is exactly the inverse of Christian charity. It is partly for this that Bossuet and other seventeenth-century Churchmen condemned comedy, a circumstance which also suggests that those who might have sympathized most fully, if not with Tartuffe, with Orgon and Madame Pernelle, must have been rare in early audiences. In comedy as in life, misfortune, deformity and affectation of many sorts were ridiculed in the seventeenth century. Ignorance, stupidity and gullibility were scourged, especially when pretentious; and the dupe, above all the cuckold or duped husband, was a figure of fun. No one has ever thought that Restoration comedy in England was exceptionally charitable, and (a Victorian legend notwithstanding) Molière's was not either.

Such themes of course may be conceived tragically. Without suggesting a further parallel, it is clear that when the hypocrite is Iago and the dupe Othello the dramatic interest is very different. Nearer to Molière. Racine's *Phèdre* and especially *Mithridate* show how themes of matrimonial disloyalty, suspicion, jealousy and hypocrisy were developed tragically. More recently, the novelist Balzac, whose medium and aims were different, has carried many of Molière's situations to a tragic fulfilment.

Comic Subject

In this play, however, the consequences seem hardly to count. They are something which a *deus ex machina* in the form of the King's Exempt can put right at the end. Secure ourselves, we may delight in watching a clever rascal hoodwink a fool just as in the medieval farce to which Molière's comedies owe so much. Our delight is redoubled at the trickster tricked, as in that most famous farce of *Maître Pierre Pathelin*, or the traitor betrayed as in an early comedy of Corneille. But the real depth and delight in *Tartuffe* is that the rascal hoodwinks himself, not through any external circumstance, but the contradictions of his own nature. It is true that without royal intervention Tartuffe would have succeeded, while Molière must have known that in life there was no Exempt to put things right; a weak ending say some, though others take it as the author's warning that in life such things end worse than at the theatre. But clearly the Exempt is a dramatic personification of a well-defined legal code which would have helped Orgon, and it would be a mistake to conclude from a 'happy' ending bound by comic convention that Tartuffe is treated superficially. Nothing could be farther from the truth. This is a play about a man who overreaches himself, a scheming mind so fixed on its goal that it misjudges its nature, which is neither clever enough, nor so free from gross humanity, to carry out the scheme. Tartuffe's hypocrisy convinces Orgon; he is impotent over himself. It is Molière's genius to have seen comedy in the power, and the limits, of religious pretence.

Yet the comic *hybris* of Tartuffe is only part of the subject. It is balanced by the credulity of Orgon and the change which takes place in him when his eyes are opened about Tartuffe. This according to the *Lettre sur la comédie de l'Imposteur* (1667) inspired by Molière is 'proprement le sujet de la pièce'. In *Tartuffe* a poetic discussion of credulity accompanies that of hypocrisy. Molière couples gullibility with pretence to complete his comic statement. Everything depends upon the blind infatuation of Orgon, which is dramatized from his first appearance on stage ('Et Tartuffe?'); and the whole climate of the play changes when Orgon is made to see what sort of man his idol really is. It is significant that upon returning home in Act I Orgon pays no attention to Dorine's unfavourable report upon Tartuffe's gluttony. Indeed, as she later tells Cléante, even when Orgon is at table with Tartuffe himself 'avec joie il l'y voit manger autant que six' (192). The fact is that Orgon admires anything that Tartuffe says or does because (like all religious people on other grounds) he is convinced to begin with that Tartuffe is holy. This is expressed perfectly by Dorine: 'Ses moindres actions lui semblent des miracles, | Et tous les mots qu'il dit sont pour lui des oracles' (197–8). Truly Tartuffe 'connaît sa dupe' (199); and it is no accident that he boasts later to Elmire: 'Et je l'ai mis au point de voir tout sans rien croire' (1526). It is the art of Molière that Tartuffe makes this boast about his power, ironically, at the moment he has overstepped it. The two themes are closed in a perfect circle: Tartuffe's confidence in his scheme is at last voiced when his infatuation with it undoes the supporting infatuation of Orgon.

The comedy of the two main characters depends then upon different attitudes toward evidence. Certain basic assumptions about its nature underlie *Tartuffe*. Of course reaction to evidence has always been a fertile field of comedy: the rogue manipulates, the fool misjudges it, as in this play Tartuffe invents the story of the flea, and Orgon mistakes it for piety, though it is accurately described as 'badinage' by Cléante (313). The ensuing rejoinders are of the utmost importance to understanding the fulcrum upon which the action turns. To Cléante's observation, Orgon replies: 'Mon frère, ce discours sent le libertinage . . .' (314), which to anyone familiar with the nature of *libertinage* and forewarned about Tartuffe must seem ridiculously wide of the mark. The point is that Orgon is unable to understand Cléante's position because his prejudice does not allow for it. He is more ready to suspect Cléante's motives than examine the evidence behind Tartuffe's story. As the former retorts:

> Voilà de vos pareils le discours ordinaire:
> Ils veulent que chacun soit aveugle comme eux.
> C'est être libertin que d'avoir de bons yeux (318–20).

Orgon would silence discussion by calling clear sight impiety.

Cléante's appeal to the evidence of what he sees has particular resonance in the 1660's. We are near the nerve of the play. Molière was ten when the Church at Rome condemned the ageing Galileo for reporting what 'de bons yeux' had seen through a telescope. Everywhere traditional beliefs were under fire; some that have survived, many that have not, such as the dictum 'Nature abhors a vacuum' which an experiment by Pascal (among others) proved to be nonsense. Indeed that Dorine couples 'miracles' in rhyme with 'oracles', the Biblical and Christian with the pagan is, though common, probably tendentious. Credulity was being advanced to explain either, and there was general concern for the effect upon faith of the new science and its approach to evidence.

The very language of Cléante's assertion that he can 'du faux avec le vrai faire la différence' (354) recalls one of the most influential books of the century, Descartes' *Discours de la Méthode* (1637), published when Molière was fifteen and relevant to any discussion of evidence in this period. In the first paragraph of his *Discours* Descartes assumes that men are all equally endowed by nature with a common sense which enables them to 'distinguer le vrai d'avec le faux'. Differences of opinion arise only, he states, because 'nous . . . ne considérons pas les mêmes choses'. The position of Cléante is very close to this, and it will be remarked that once Orgon can be forced to consider the facts about Tartuffe he comes to agree with his family. He responds no longer to his obsession, but to the 'témoignage' (1549) of what he has himself seen and heard. Then with characteristic self-confidence, his rôle reversed, he is as insistent upon this evidence as if he had never been mistaken: 'Je l'ai vu, dis-je, vu, de mes propres yeux vu, | Ce qu'on appelle vu . . .' (1676–7). The obstinacy of his mother as he attempts to persuade and her tiresome appeal to irrelevant opinion reinforces Orgon's comic reversal.

This suggests one of the ways in which Molière's comedy goes deeper than Descartes' purely rational approach to evidence. For the total meaning of the play is not limited to the position of Cléante. It embraces not only the facts involved in evidence, but the subconscious attituds ewhich prevent our considering the same facts. Madame Perneell in the last act extends the portrait in Orgon of that comic tendency in human nature to resist unpleasant evidence, while we see in his impatience and scarcely diminished self-satisfaction some of the background of his credulity. At a time when most philosophers were devoted to a 'rational' explanation of human behaviour and theologians often interpreted the workings of the subconscious as interference by devils, Molière's mimetic art cast light upon the hidden reaches of the heart: '. . . on est aisément dupé par ce qu'on aime, | Et l'amour-propre engage à se tromper soi-même' (1357–8). For the comic force of Elmire's *sententiae* is their ambivalence. What she says to Orgon before unmasking Tartuffe she is also saying about him. There is double reference, to Orgon and to the audience; and Molière uses it once more to bind up his subject. In his conception pretence and gullibility are not manifested separately. The same words which foretell gullibility behind Tartuffe's pretence also imply pretence in the gullible Orgon, which is hardly the less real for being unrecognized.

It is some years since the late Professor Auerbach showed that Orgon's delusion of piety serves mainly to indulge the unavowed instinct of the family tyrant. 'He loves Tartuffe and lets himself be duped by him because Tartuffe makes it possible for him to satisfy his instinctive urge to tyrannize over and torment his family' (p. 318). 'Faire enrager le monde est ma plus grande joie', exclaims Orgon as he prepares to disinherit Damis (1173). Without the pretence of piety Orgon would never have dared say such a thing, nor later: 'Je porte en ce contrat de quoi vous faire rire' (1277). For he says more than he means, just as Molière's imaginary invalid (in a scene which strongly resembles Orgon's quarrel with Dorine in II, ii) is made to blurt out: 'je suis méchant quand je veux'. (*Cf.* 373, 1126, 1128–30, 1175, and 1184.) Over against his portrait of the man who consciously exploits piety, Molière ingeniously shows how it is used unconsciously to remove the social and family obstacles to what we now call sadism. The conscious mask of Tartuffe is made to reveal the subconscious mask of Orgon, together with that deeply ingrained 'amour-propre' which impels them both and finally trips them up. It is the peculiar triumph of Molière that, conscious or subconscious, the mask of piety does not conceal, but *shows* the man.

Sources

Examination of Molière's sources confirms the originality of his achievement, which often lies in what has been added, suppressed or altered. Neither his ideas nor his situations as such are especially new. They fit into well-defined traditions of theatrical art and humanist thought. His originality lies rather in their fusion. It is in a new concentration, inversion, redoubling of themes which allows them to be seen from a new angle. The mask discussed figuratively above, for example, had been a common stage-property earlier in the century. Molière (after Corneille) adapts the mask to a mask of words, and allusions to the property (334, 1374) contain an image highly suggestive in interpreting the rôle of Tartuffe. But in Molière the verbal mask is infinitely more varied. Not only does Tartuffe make lies mask truth, but at the end of Act III he uses truth itself as a mask (1074 ff.). It has been observed likewise that Tartuffe and Orgon retain something of the rogue and the fool of medieval farce, and this source sheds light upon their comic relationship, but more importantly upon the workings of Molière's comic art in which the fool is foolish as a pretext to roguery and the rogue is trapped by his foolishness. This is at once more complex and more coherent, and utterly original.

There are apparently many sources for Tartuffe. His name comes from the Italian 'tartufulo', meaning 'truffe' in French or truffle. The verb 'truffer' could mean 'tromper', and 'truffeur' could mean 'trompeur'. But 'truffe' seems also to have been used of a bulbous nose (*cf.* 'Oui, c'est un beau museau', 560). A literary source has been suggested for Tartuffe in the novel literature of the period, then widely read though now largely forgotten: a hypocrite in D'Audiguier's *Amours d'Aristandre et de Cléonice* (1624). The name Tartuffe recalls Montufar in the *Hypocrites* of Scarron, who like so many contemporaries adapted his subject from a Spanish original. This confirms that its sound is important, and when Molière altered his title for a single performance in 1667 he chose the name 'Panulphe'. La Bruyère's (later) hypocrite in *De la Mode* has the analogous name 'Onuphre'. But Tartuffe has also assimilated other traditional types. His gluttony suggests the Parasite or hanger-on of Latin and Renaissance comedy. He may partake also of the *miles gloriosus* or braggart soldier ('Il est de faux dévots ainsi que de faux braves', 326), the type which boasts without matching deed to word.

Orgon also is a 'fanfaron' of devotion. He is a fool; but on another level he is the man who gets things wrong because he is visionary rather than simply foolish. It is a contrived foolishness in which Orgon unwittingly collaborates at his own deception. He might be called a 'dévot ridicule', because like the *précieuses* of Molière's farce he imitates the externals of piety without understanding its inner meaning. He is a 'dévot imaginaire', successor to Sganarelle, Molière's 'cocu imaginaire', fancying himself pious as Sganarelle imagines himself cuckolded. Or if we may look forward to a later play, Orgon may be seen as a 'bourgeois gentilhomme' of devotion, a visionary who abandons the solid bourgeois qualities of family affection for imaginary mystic qualities which are as much a misfit upon Orgon as the would-be nobleman's outlandish imitation of aristocratic costume and manners. For his acts all belie his delusion.

Clearly Molière's own earlier works are an important 'source'. Two things are especially notable about *Tartuffe* in his career: a broadening of comic vision, and its heavy satiric content. In comparison with his earlier plays, both characters and comic structure are appreciably more complex. Earlier Molière had concentrated upon one or two rôles only. These are fully characterized in the better plays, but the same is hardly true of supporting rôles. In *Tartuffe* for the first time, as Professor Adam remarks, we have a fully drawn bourgeois interior (III, 319). There is a notable advance in realism of both setting and cast. Supporting rôles are given individual characterization, and with minor exceptions all have dramatic life in flesh and blood. There is still concentration upon the principals, Tartuffe and Orgon, but in terms of comic relationships which are at once more complex and more human. Molière is seeking a new comedy independent of the stock comic types, which in *Tartuffe* are not abandoned, but developed and fulfilled.

Intentions

As originally performed in three acts in 1664, *Tartuffe* followed the quarrel over *L'Ecole des Femmes* in the course of which Molière had discussed his dramatic art in two plays: *La Critique de l'Ecole des Femmes* and *L'Impromptu de Versailles*. In the former the poet's spokesmen refer to comedy as a 'public mirror', a glass held up before the public to reflect a true portrait of the times. That is to say, a stylized portrait, in the contemporary tradition of portraiture. Molière's assumption in this matter would be the same as that of La Rochefoucauld: 'Les seules bonnes copies sont celles qui nous font voir le ridicule des méchants originaux'. A satirical intention is admitted, and Molière, through his chief spokesman, appeals to the 'bons yeux' and the 'bon sens naturel' of the Court. Moral and aesthetic considerations are not overlooked, but we are asked whether in comedy 'la grande règle de toutes les règles n'est pas de plaire'.

In *Tartuffe*, however, there is a change of emphasis. The desire to please is coupled with a far more evident mission to correct what Molière considered anti-social abuses: possibly exasperation with devout attacks upon *L'Ecole des Femmes* prompted Molière in his satire of hypocrisy. The first *Placet* written in defence of *Tartuffe* begins: 'Le devoir de la comédie étant de corriger les hommes en les divertissant . . .' Throughout the seventeenth century it was said that comedy, like the satire of Horace, 'castigat ridendo mores'. Molière aims in *Tartuffe* at just such 'serious laughter'; and in attacking the vices of his century through ridicule, he denies that any of them should be given the privilege of immunity, not even hypocrisy. But there is more than that. Orgon is sincere enough (if that is the word where there seems to be so little self-knowledge), and he is ridiculed as well as Tartuffe. Hypocrisy is not then really the vital question, and it seems likely that the service which Molière wished to render the 'honnêtes gens' of his century included ridicule not only of the 'faux dévot', but also of that 'cabale' of perfectly sincere, but intolerant, men who sought among other works of piety to close the theatre. The most distinguished enemies of *Tartuffe* were dedicated Churchmen like the Archbishop Hardouin de Péréfixe, Bourdaloue and Bossuet. It is not at all clear that the Président de Lamoignon, who banned *Tartuffe*, was a hypocrite, though it seems likely that the Compagnie du Saint-Sacrement of which he was a member came at least indirectly under Molière's comic lash. Cléante alludes to the 'cabale' (397).

It should not be forgotten, moreover, that the preface and 'placets' of *Tartuffe* are polemical works. Molière's interest was not to express everything he thought about his play, but to stress conventional arguments which were likely to win permission to perform it. Nor perhaps is what Molière, the man, intended so important a question, but rather what Molière, the playwright, wrote. It is significant, however, that he defended his work through five bitter years of controversy and disappointment when at least one pamphleteer wanted to burn him alive, a threat the more meaningful to Parisians in 1664 who the year before had witnessed Simon Morin burned for heresy upon the order of the same Président de Lamoignon who banned *Tartuffe*. Neither the desire to profit from a large gate, nor a satirical intent, fully explains Molière's tenacity, but the sense that he had created a work of lasting beauty which he would not allow to be suppressed.

Changes

Molière's fight for *Tartuffe*, which occupied nearly five years at the peak of his career, is itself a sombre episode of more than ordinary interest in its own right and in the genesis of the text we possess. The problems involved are too complicated, if not too speculative, for full discussion here. But the main points warrant attention. We know that when it was first performed at Versailles, on May 12, 1664, *Tartuffe* had only three acts and that Louis XIV found it a 'comédie fort divertissante'. It seems to have been something of a farce and perhaps bolder in its conception than the five-act 'comédie de caractère' which we now have, performed and published in 1669. The question is whether the three acts originally performed constituted a complete play, analogous say to Molière's *George Dandin*, or only three acts of an unfinished play in five acts. Excellent scholars, including Professor Adam of the Sorbonne, think that it was unfinished. An earlier Sorbonne professor and specialist in Molière, however, G. Michaut, maintained convincingly that *Tartuffe* as first performed was a finished play.[1] It would have ended near the end of the present Act III, that is, at the moment when Orgon, refusing the evidence of his eyes, tells Tartuffe to frequent Elmire: 'Et je veux qu'à toute heure avec elle on vous voie' (1174). The curtain would close upon Orgon as a potential *cocu*.

[1] G. Michaut, *Les Luttes de Molière*, Paris, 1925, pp. 56 ff.

More recently, John Cairncross has argued in a special study of the question that, although Michaut was right to conclude that the three-act play first performed was a finished one, he was wrong to assume that it ended with Act III. Instead he considers that the first *Tartuffe* 'was complete in three acts which are roughly identical with Acts I, III and IV of the present play, that Mariane and Valère (who more or less monopolize Act II) did not exist originally. . . .'[1] The love interest would have been supplied by Damis' projected marriage, and the play would have ended with the exposure of Tartuffe near the end of Act IV or 'just possibly' with the comic disbelief of Madame Pernelle (now V, iii). The important difference from Michaut's position obviously is that in such a play, as in the present one, Tartuffe would not have succeeded. The proposed marriage of Tartuffe to Mariane, the 'dépit amoureux' which ends Act II (and closely resembles a scene in an earlier play of that title by Molière), the 'cassette' which joins Act IV to Act V, as of course most (if not all) of the last act, would have been added in 1665 or 1666. Mr. Cairncross makes no claim that the evidence on these points is conclusive, but he does suggest that such an historical reading would be useful in explaining what to him and others have seemed weaknesses in the structure of the play. These include the 'dépit amoureux' and somewhat misleading pretexts suggested by Dorine at the end of Act II, the 'cassette' introduced without preparation at the very end of Act IV, the sinister behaviour of Tartuffe in the last act (said to be out of keeping with farcical gluttony earlier in the play), and the royal intervention. Michaut had also regarded most of Act II as an addition, especially the 'dépit amoureux', but his 'additions' would include also such vital scenes in the present comedy as the one between Tartuffe and Elmire with Orgon under the table (IV, v).

Rather more is known of an intermediate stage in the development of *Tartuffe*. We know that a five-act comedy was read and

[1] John Cairncross, *New Light on Molière*, Geneva, 1956, p. 3.

performed privately in 1664 and 1665, but for the first public performance in Paris, August 5, 1667, Molière renamed his play *Panulphe*, dressed his impostor as a man of the world rather than in the semi-ecclesiastical garb of the first and final versions, and apparently attenuated certain other objectionable elements. Production was nevertheless interrupted after a single performance. However, the *Lettre sur la Comédie de l'Imposteur*, inspired, perhaps partly written, by Molière himself and published in the same year, gives a very full notion of its staging and content to which critics of even the definitive text are indebted. As the commentary and paraphrasing are very detailed, certain omissions suggest noteworthy changes in the final text, such as Tartuffe's flea (I, v) and Orgon's attempt to slap Dorine (II, ii). Cléante seems also to have had a somewhat more active rôle, but not so long a discussion of true and false piety in I, v, 'obviously added', according to Mr. Cairncross, 'in an apologetic intent' (p. 41).

Whatever the reasons for Molière's changes (and if some were polemical, others were certainly dramatic and literary), they now form part of the play, first performed in February 1669, under the original title and with Tartuffe again in black. The text published later the same year is the only one we have. Also it is with this text that the following remarks on structure and style are concerned. Clearly if tirades are added with 'apologetic intent', the play becomes to that extent apologetic. One may approve or deplore the change. That is criticism, and the background of the change is relevant. One may even argue that such tirades are as external to the real play as the preface, reflecting not so much what Molière wished to stage as part of a compromise necessary to stage his play at all. The inclusion of such scenes as the 'dépit amoureux' and the final intervention of the King through his Exempt have likewise been criticized as padding and flattery. The following analyses, however, are based upon the finished literary artefact. Their aim is less to criticize than to interpret Molière's play. It is not to evaluate the alternative ways in which he might have built a comedy, but to examine the unique values in the construction of this one.

2. *Structure*

Asked towards the end of his life how a play should be constructed, Goethe replied that it should be symbolic. 'That is to say, each situation must be important in itself and lead toward something more important still.' In this respect, he adds, *Tartuffe* is a splendid model. Its exposition is unique. Everything from the first scene is of great consequence and foreshadows something greater. For it is not simply the events of a play that matter, Goethe implies, but the order and rhythm in which they are presented. That is the subject of this chapter.

Act I

The reader may have wondered among others things why a play entitled *Tartuffe* begins with the departure of Madame Pernelle, who does not reappear until the very end, while the impostor himself is withheld until the third act. Goethe's remarks suggest the answer. The play opens upon a crisis. We are shown the remarkable effects of Tartuffe, which in turn stimulate interest in their cause. The playwright uses the first scenes at once to arouse our curiosity and to prepare our acceptance of such an extraordinary figure.

The setting places us in what seems to be a perfectly ordinary bourgeois household. But it is full of an ominous animation. We are plunged into the action by the very haste of the actresses. Who is this drab old lady, and why is she off in such high dudgeon? (It is far less clear to the spectator than to the reader for whom the characters are identified, though the former has the advantage of seeing that Madame Pernelle's clothes are in sharp contrast with the fashionable attire of Elmire, Damis,

Mariane and Cléante. Madame Pernelle was originally played by a male actor.)

As the others crowd around, Madame Pernelle complains that she is 'contrariée' in everything; she cuts off anyone else who tries to speak, but all in such a way that the relationships become clear. It is for the spectator, for example, that Madame Pernelle adds in rebuking Damis:

> C'est moi qui vous le dis, qui suis votre grand'mère;
> Et j'ai prédit cent fois à mon fils, votre père . . . (17–18).

Then, when everyone has been presented, we come to the heart of the matter: Tartuffe, the impostor promised in the subtitle. This is what divides the household.

For Madame Pernelle: 'C'est un homme de bien, qu'il faut que l'on écoute' (42). But listen to Tartuffe is precisely what none of the rest is prepared to do. To Damis, Madame Pernelle's 'homme de bien' is a 'cagot de critique' (45), and to Dorine a shoeless beggar who has forgotten his place. When Madame Pernelle observes, in reference to his hostility to visitors, that '. . . l'intérêt du Ciel est tout ce qui le pousse' (78), Dorine has an alternative explanation: 'Je crois que de Madame il est, ma foi, jaloux' (84). Thus from the first we are advised to look to the man beneath the mask, and the amorous inclination of Tartuffe is presented with his imposture.

Madame Pernelle, however, prefers to consider on this question, not whether the other evidence on Tartuffe supports the ostensible motive for his words, but that his words are repeated elsewhere: 'Ce n'est pas lui tout seul qui blâme ces visites' (86). This introduces the theme of credulity, prefiguring the great scene of Act III in which Orgon refuses to credit Damis' denunciation of Tartuffe ('Je sais bien quel motif à l'attaquer t'oblige', 1118) and Madame Pernelle's own prejudice upon her return in Act V ('Les gens de bien sont enviés toujours', 1659). It is the comedy of the general maxim misapplied. Content with its introduction here, Molière allows his characters to engage in a spirited discussion which informs the spectator that the criticized visits are of a sort which no frequenter of the theatre could possibly blame. It is cut short by Cléante's laughing at the strictures of Madame Pernelle, who exits boxing Flipote's ears.

Now let us examine what we have seen. To begin with, the scene is animated. It begins in a rush and ends with a blow. Young people are defending what must seem to the audience innocent pleasure against a frightfully unsmart old lady who loses her temper. We do not see Tartuffe, but we hear a great deal about him in this dispute. This is important, because obviously our opinion of Tartuffe will be influenced by our judgement of these contestants: in his absence he will be judged first by association. How Madame Pernelle is presented thus matters enormously, for she is Tartuffe's only champion. (He will never have more than one on stage at a time.) Madame Pernelle is devout. She might have been shown in prayer. Instead she is found in a rage. She must have sympathetic friends; she is discovered among enemies. She is Orgon's mother; we meet her as Elmire's mother-in-law. Elmire is civil, behaving as she should in her own home; Madame Pernelle is rude to her hostess. Having questioned her austerity, Cléante laughs good-naturedly, whereas Madame Pernelle praises the piety of Tartuffe and boxes her servant's ears. Surely all this weights the scales against the 'dévot personnage'.

Madame Pernelle's blow also dramatizes a disposition to violence which is important in the Orgon family psychology and at the same time presents an image of a universal comic phenomenon. Her violence anticipates the 'emportement' alike of her grandson Damis, who at the opening of Act III threatens as usual 'quelque coup de ma tête' (826), and of her son Orgon, who at the end of the same act is found shouting: 'Un bâton! un bâton!' (1135). 'Like father, like son', the adage has it. The theme is very old, but as it recurs in this play it takes on a special and deeply comic significance. Madame Pernelle's reaction represents a very human inclination to answer compelling argument by force or flight. It foreshadows Orgon's reply later in this act to Cléante's distinction between true and false piety: 'Monsieur mon cher beau-frère, avez-vous tout dit?' (408). It looks forward to the farcical scene in Act II in which Orgon attempts to discuss his daughter's marriage while preparing to strike Dorine (570–84), and to Tartuffe's brusqueness with Cléante in Act IV (1266). In these and similar situations, the reaction is comic on many levels. It is first of all irrelevant, like Madame Pernelle's failure in Act V to grasp the point of Orgon's exposure of Tartuffe, and thus ludicrously inadequate to the circumstances. It represents also (in Bergsonian terms) the abrupt intrusion of the physical upon the moral, as when a lecturer stumbles against the podium, and doubly comic for Orgon and Madame Pernelle because incongruous with their self-righteousness. Molière has also skilfully balanced his structure by allowing the violence of his devout personages to overflow into the sympathetic character of Damis.

Nor is it by accident that when the family escort Madame Pernelle to the door, Tartuffe's most outspoken enemy, Dorine, is left to explain his relationship with her absent master to Cléante, who as the brother of Elmire is something of a stranger to the household and consequently useful to the exposition. Up to now we have heard little of Orgon; but as the mother leaves, Dorine primes us for the son:

> Oh! vraiment tout cela n'est rien au prix du fils,
> Et si vous l'aviez vu, vous diriez: 'C'est bien pis!' (179–80).

We are being made to anticipate (and so accept) Orgon's extravagance. What can the man be like who is said to love Tartuffe 'cent fois plus qu'il ne fait mère, fils, fille, et femme' (186)? Our curiosity should be sufficiently aroused to cover the coincidence of his return.

For hardly has Dorine given a few particulars upon Tartuffe when Elmire, Mariane and Damis re-enter announcing Orgon's return after two days' absence. Damis takes barely the time to ask Cléante's intercession on behalf of Valère's engagement to Mariane. Then wife, son and daughter scatter, leaving the brother-in-law and servant to greet the returned master. In this way Molière dramatizes the strain upon family ties at which Dorine had just hinted, setting the stage for his own entry as Orgon.

It may help at this point to recall that in the convention followed by Molière a scene automatically ends whenever an actor enters or exits, but that at least one actor is always left on stage (as now). This is less to obtain a formal 'liaison de scènes' than to prevent the spectators (some of whom were likely to be seated or even standing on the stage itself) from becoming more than usually restless. If in this way the return of Orgon is brought improbably near the departure of Madame Pernelle (there is no curtain drop to indicate the passing of a vague amount of time), the quiet conversation between Cléante and Dorine offers an interlude of repose between the hurly-burly of the opening scene and the farce of Orgon's entrance.

It is a *tour de force*. We have been warned of Orgon's infatuation; here we see it. Four times Dorine attempts to describe to Orgon his wife's illness. Each time his preoccupation springs forward: 'Et Tartuffe?' And as faultlessly as the question had sprung to his lips, the identical term of endearment falls mechanically into place at the answer: 'Le pauvre homme!' It is a sort of *leitmotif* of Orgon infatuated. He repeats it himself at the very end of Act III when Tartuffe has persuaded him that Damis' true denunciation is a false calumny deserving disinheritance (1183). Dorine crowns with it Orgon's account of Tartuffe's misdeeds to Madame Pernelle in Act V (1657). Thus even in the tensest moments Orgon retains something of the reassuring qualities of the clown.

Critics have objected that this high-spirited scene is unrealistic: people do not ordinarily repeat things so obviously as Orgon. Others maintain that the subject deserves a more serious treatment. These objections arise, however, from arbitrary conceptions of what constitutes dramatic art and the nature of its meaning. In this scene we are in full comic convention; and it must be examined, not as a 'slice of life', but as part of a work of art. The social disorientation of the preoccupied man is common enough as a natural phenomenon (it is the background of almost all jokes about the absent-minded professor). But in nature it rarely takes so studied a form. The image which Molière offers of it is concentrated and heightened. It is that of the artist rather than the photographer. Orgon's inflexible responses dramatize the rigidity of his absorption in Tartuffe. The human in Orgon has been overlaid with the jack-in-the-box of his infatuation. It springs up in exactly the same mechanical way no matter which side is touched. Or in terms nearer the sources of Molière, the man is a puppet to his passion and gives the same stiff jerk whenever the central string is pulled. This scene is the exterior, perceptible form of a moral inflexibility.

Molière never bungled preparations. That is one of the reasons why this scene comes fourth instead of first. By insensible degrees he has brought us from the commonplace reality of a contemporary setting to this high degree of stylization. The genius of the playwright is as evident in the preparation and placing of such a scene as in its technical elaboration. For not only has Dorine told us to expect an infatuated Orgon; the departure of Madame Pernelle has prefigured her son's entry in an unobtrusive, but concrete and technically demonstrable way.

In the opening scene, each word addressed to Madame Pernelle releases the expression of a deep-seated grudge. The formula of address varies ('Si . . .', 'Mais . . .', 'Je crois . . .', 'Mais, ma mère . . .', 'Mais, Madame, après tout . . .'); the reaction retains the same pattern. Her preoccupation is not so stylized in its presentation. It is less concentrated, because we see it as a grievance against each of five characters rather than obsession with one. Our need for orientation in the play and the presence of many characters on stage also tend to obscure the mechanics of the scene. Yet all the elements of infatuation are there. Upon Orgon's entry, the poet isolates this human phenomenon. Extraneous matter is, as it were, cleared away so that we may concentrate upon its simplest, its eternal, its classical state. In musical terms, the thematic material of the introduction is triumphantly re-stated in its basic form.

When Dorine leaves the stage, however, there is a change of mood. Questioned by Cléante, Orgon likes nothing better than to discourse upon Tartuffe. But he is greatly annoyed that Cléante fails to take him seriously. From the particular then the discussion shifts to the general, embracing soon all the vast question of true *versus* false devotion. The action of the play is thereby situated at the centre of a vibrant moral controversy. A relevance to life is suggested in the very nature of the questions raised, and lest the audience misconceive his satire Molière carefully limits it. Cléante indeed denounces, in a set speech of more than fifty lines developed under contemporary rules of rhetoric and superbly articulate, those 'qui savent ajuster leur zèle avec leurs vices' (373). This is of more than ordinary interest as in the preface to *Tartuffe*, one of the rare texts in which Molière writes personally of his dramatic intentions, he states that he employed '. . . tout l'art et tous les soins qu'il m'a été possible pour bien distinguer le personnage de l'Hypocrite d'avec celui du vrai Dévot'. We are thus invited to see in this passage an example of that 'sublime ventriloquism' whereby dramatic authors sometimes deliver directly a 'thesis' also implied by the action.

But the play is ordered so that at the end of this speech it falls to Cléante to ask a favour. Having spoken his mind, he must now negotiate with a ruffled Orgon; and the final scene of this act may be nearer the nerve of the play than the appended discourse. This exchange is a brilliant staging of the position of any devout person (not simply the hypocrite because it is Orgon here) who finds his pledged word in conflict with his inspiration. At the same time the comic inversion implied by the necessity to ask again, and in these circumstances, what has already been promised tends to relax the philosophic tension of the preceding exchange, while the doubt now raised about the future of Mariane rekindles dramatic interest. Will Orgon honour his promise to Valère? Orgon's attitude in this scene involves not only the fate of the young couple, but the very nature of piety. We are given a touchstone by which to test the devoutness of the man who, questioned upon a solemn obligation, will undertake to perform only 'ce que le Ciel voudra' (423). It is a measure of Molière's distinction that a device to hold our attention also dramatizes the deepest meaning of the play.

Act II

Molière does not hold us long in suspense. Mariane is to marry ... Tartuffe. Before making his announcement, however, Orgon inspects an antechamber (428–30). It is easy to see that this prepares a hiding place for Damis in the following act. But the gesture is far more significant as preparing the atmosphere of the succeeding acts. In no more dramatic way could Molière convey the distrust which Tartuffe has brought into the house. An atmosphere of suspicion pervades the play. Dramatic events are unfolded against a sombre background of espionage and suspicion which gives them depth in space as well as time. Partly for this *Tartuffe* has been called, perhaps inaptly, a 'dark comedy'. For however gloomy the background, the treatment is gloriously comic.

This is accomplished, it seems to me, partly by the ambivalence of the dramatic symbols themselves. In this one, for example, distrust is not the only motif introduced. Orgon's gesture contains also the comic theme of useless precaution. Interruption comes from Dorine, not the antechamber, which will not be inspected when it contains a spy. There may also be an element of guilty conscience from lingering paternal affection (*cf.* 1293). The inspection creates at once the sombre atmosphere required for Orgon's inhuman announcement and foreshadows the comic futility of a scheme erected against human nature.

Mariane is coaxed to agree to say whatever Orgon wishes about Tartuffe, but she had hardly reckoned to say she would marry him:

> Il n'en est rien, mon père, je vous jure.
> Pourquoi me faire dire une telle imposture? (449–50).

Her naïve recoil from such an unutterable 'imposture' is made to describe her father's scheme. His reply is noteworthy: 'Mais je veux que cela soit une vérité'. It appears to give (inadvertent?) expression to two ideas: Orgon will put his own wish before his daughter's happiness ('je veux . . .'), but rather than admit this to himself he will call the false true ('. . . que cela soit une vérité'). A few lines later the possessive adjectives are eloquent upon the first point: 'Oui, je prétends, ma fille, | Unir par *votre* hymen Tartuffe à *ma* famille' (453–4). It is Dorine who spells out the comic implications of this attitude two scenes later. She advises Mariane to say to Orgon:

> . . . qu'un cœur n'aime point par autrui,
> Que vous vous mariez pour vous, non pas pour lui (591–2).

We are introduced at the same moment to Orgon's selfish scheme and his tendency to mask unpalatable fact. There is a double reference in Mariane's word 'imposture' which suggests that Tartuffe is not the only impostor. The language of the play, like its symbols, is ambivalent.

But the effects are varied. The stealthy entrance of Dorine now turns discussion into farce, varying the rhythm and offering further comic insight into the proposal of Orgon. Dorine herself offers a key to interpretation of this scene when she later asks Mariane:

> Avez-vous donc perdu, dites-moi, la parole,
> Et faut-il qu'en ceci je fasse votre rôle? (585–6).

However free the speech permitted a faithful servant, there is comic inversion in the fact that she speaks to her master as a headstrong daughter might while the daughter remains silent. Speech is Dorine's weapon. It is with 'la parole' that she adroitly boxes Orgon into a corner where he can only blurt out what is deeply true, but inadmissible: 'Je ne veux pas qu'on m'aime' (545). She points to the contradiction between his anger and supposed piety. Then, told to remain silent, she observes: 'Soit. Mais, ne disant mot, je ne pense pas moins' (555). Orgon does not fancy hearing truths he would prefer to ignore; Dorine's remark serves to show that changing the label does not alter the contents. When she speaks up again, as if impelled, it is upon the pretence that she is speaking to herself, a frequent comic device which is also a poetic way of expressing the fact that words designed to convey meaning have not 'got across'.

Dorine had dwelt upon *cocuage* as a possible result of Mariane's marrying Tartuffe; in the following scene suicide is broached as a possible reaction. But Dorine treats it (615–17) with irony similar to that which she uses later in the scene to predict provincial life for Mariane as Madame Tartuffe. The moral consequences of Orgon's 'pious' intentions are explored, and in the course of conversation the depth of Mariane's attachment to Valère is brought out against a background of further satire of Tartuffe. The irony of Dorine has just given way to a sense of urgency injected by Mariane's return to the idea of suicide, when enters . . . Valère.

Instead of action, we have now a 'dépit amoureux'. This scene has been called superfluous—an irrelevant digression intended merely to fill out Act II while we await the entry of Tartuffe. Yet the 'dépit amoureux' dramatizes the moral effect of Orgon's infatuation upon the young people and continues also the comic theme of inconsequential behaviour. They dispute when they should act. A closer examination reveals moreover that we are led deeper into the comic discrepancies of language. 'Que sais-je si le cœur a parlé par la bouche . . .?', asks Dorine in the preceding scene (605). In this one we are shown one of the situations in which it does not. As such it fits into a series of scenes in which

Orgon first says more than he means (ii), Dorine ironically expresses the contrary of her thought in order to strengthen Mariane's resistance (iii), and the lovers speak against their hearts through wounded pride. By any definition of structure larger than intrigue itself, the relationship of language to dramatic fact is central to the conception of this play; and this sequence leads to the next situation in which the hypocrite speaks deliberately to deceive. This scene is not then simply an 'hors d'œuvre' which everyone has found independently pleasing, but a relevant component of Molière's study in the comic use of language.

Moreover, if now we look at *Tartuffe* as a poetic discussion of the contrived and the instinctive, we may see in these lovers, who have all the symbolic force of a long tradition, a dramatized resistance to Orgon's inhuman scheme. However inexpertly, whatever is human and alive in their passion finally resists, Tartuffe's plot. The naïve resistance which Dorine had first assumed for Mariane, then recommended to her, here is realized. Instinct carries the day. Before Tartuffe's calculations are undone by his instinctive passion for Elmire, the resilience of love is as it were personified in Mariane and Valère. The instinctive is outwardly, before inwardly, opposed to the calculations of the faux dévots'. The conclusion also offers an interval of hope between the misgiving that closed Act I and the sombre opening of Act III.

Act III

Before we are at last allowed to see the impostor in action, the stage is skilfully set. In a brief introductory scene, we are reminded of the 'emportement' of Damis and of Tartuffe's inclination for Elmire. Damis is a 'fâcheux' (852) whose interference will destroy momentarily what may be called the limited objective of Elmire, to win Tartuffe's opposition to marriage with Mariane. But his presence on stage assures limits to Tartuffe's progress in seduction while providing a comic situation in which Tartuffe's private confession is overheard by his enemy.

The first words of Tartuffe stamp his rôle as firmly as Orgon was stamped on first appearance by repetition of his name: 'Laurent, serrez ma haire avec ma discipline' (853). The hypocrite is evident in Tartuffe from the moment he appears. Never, as Molière observes in his preface, is the spectator in any doubt. Appearing for the first time after two full acts' preparation, Tartuffe is at once obliged and able to proffer some notable extravagance. 'Car un caractère de cette force tomberait', reads the *Lettre sur la comédie de l'Imposteur*, 's'il paraissait sans faire d'abord un jeu digne de lui, ce qui ne se pouvait que dans le fort de l'action.' The first gestures of Tartuffe derive from and fulfil a long expectation. It is no accident that they concern Dorine, his avowed and outspoken enemy, whose sharp remarks offer (as at the *début* of Orgon) a foil against which Tartuffe is presented. Catching sight of Dorine, Tartuffe promptly dons the mask of asceticism. But it requires only the message from Elmire to loosen Tartuffe's mask: 'Comme il se radoucit!' (875). Love momentarily disconcerts 'l'âme de toutes la mieux concertée'.

Everything turns then upon Tartuffe's first interview with Elmire. If there has never been any doubt about Tartuffe's hypocrisy, it is now possible to understand his success. For he is prodigiously eloquent. Straightaway he addresses to Elmire two quatrains which might almost be taken for the madrigals then popular, here expressing pious sentiment in gallant form. But soon a note of ambiguity is introduced:

Elmire.
Pour moi, ce que je veux, c'est un mot d'entretien,
Où tout votre cœur s'ouvre, et ne me cache rien.
Tartuffe.
Et je ne veux aussi pour grâce singulière
Que montrer à vos yeux mon âme toute entière (903–6).

Expressions like 'ne me cache rien' and 'grâce singulière' must have one meaning for the speaker, another for the listener, and yet another for the alerted spectator.

Tartuffe's declaration begins with what seems to be an involuntary gesture. He seizes Elmire's hand, then allows his own to drop to her knee. Questioned about it, he can only reply unconvincingly: 'Je tâte votre habit: l'étoffe en est moelleuse' (917). To readjust the mask of piety, any pretext serves. There is nothing that Tartuffe wants more than to lay it aside, but he must take care how he does so. It is by a parody of the liturgy: by an argument couched in comically equivocal terms he claims to admire in Elmire 'l'auteur de la nature' (942). Her surprise at such a declaration from so 'devout' a man prepares a speech by Tartuffe which occupies what may be called the structural centre of the comedy. That is to say, not only does the speech occur in the physical centre of the text, which is important, but it also contains the principal comic themes of *Tartuffe*.

These are expressed at the beginning and the end. The first deals with the instinctive nature of Tartuffe's love for Elmire, earlier foreshadowed and foreshadowing his undoing:

> Ah! pour être dévot, je n'en suis pas moins homme;
> Et lorsqu'on vient à voir vos célestes appas,
> Un cœur se laisse prendre, et ne raisonne pas (966–8).

Orgon was right: 'c'est . . . un homme enfin' (272). Tartuffe has said more than he means, and no mask can alter the fact here inadvertently expressed. The accident of his affection for Elmire ('vient à voir') is sufficient to put the mask aside. Instinct has undone calculation. The vertical man is tripping upon the horizontal one.

Another theme is the hypocrisy which the master of it explains at the end of the same speech. A mask of discretion will, he boasts, permit 'de l'amour sans scandale et du plaisir sans peur' (1000), a suggestive formula which by implication denies a provident deity and prepares the hypocrite's cynical assertion in the corresponding scene of Act IV:

> Et le mal n'est jamais que dans l'éclat qu'on fait;

Le scandale du monde est ce qui fait l'offense,
Et ce n'est pas pécher que pécher en silence (1504–6).

The impostor, more than he reckoned, is showing his 'âme toute entière'. We are allowed to see the evil which he represents and hear him explain it. This is not a character about whom 'right you are if you think you are'. Molière takes the trouble to tell us: 'c'est un scélérat qui parle', dispelling any notion that the author is speaking through this rôle. But there is a special irony in the fact that the comedy is constructed so that either time Tartuffe is overheard when he makes his outrageous assertion about sin in secrecy, here by Damis, later by Orgon.

Damis' interference at this point, however, is a stroke of pure theatrical genius. In the first place, if Tartuffe has laid bare his heart, Elmire has not yet had time to reciprocate, nor even to settle the matter of Tartuffe's marriage to Mariane. We know that Elmire is rather isolated in her own home. Her husband is infatuated with Tartuffe and in any case seems to be a good deal older with little time for the parties and balls which Elmire likes. Madame Pernelle is of course her enemy, Damis is not especially sympathetic to her, and she seems to have no especially cordial relationship with her step-daughter. The first scenes show that Cléante is something of a stranger to the house, and Dorine is committed first of all to the interests of Orgon and his children. Indeed there seems to be no person in the play with whom she can lay bare her heart, as evidenced by the fact that nowhere except with Tartuffe or in preparing to trap him does she speak privately with anyone. Some critics have wondered whether in the circumstances she has no ulterior motive in opposing the marriage of Mariane. Certain of her expressions have seemed somewhat suspect, as her reply to Tartuffe's assurances of discretion (1001–2). Damis also seems a bit suspicious about her reaction (*cf.* 1035). We know too that *cocuage* was a favourite comic theme with Molière, and it may be that the play originally ended with Orgon's encouraging Tartuffe to frequent his wife.

Then Molière's women often follow instinct and we know that Charpy de Sainte-Croix passed as a seducer. Yet it is doubtful that Elmire should appear to encourage Tartuffe in this scene. Though there is doubtless comedy in the potential *cocuage* of Orgon, successor to Sganarelle and Arnolphe, Tartuffe seems too gross and socially too *gauche* to tempt Elmire.

But there is another consequence to Damis' attempt to unmask Tartuffe. He has not realized the danger, and the comic possibilities, of confronting Tartuffe after his heart has been laid bare only before the audience and those characters who suspected him already. The truth is one thing, to convince another. Also when Orgon enters (and Elmire leaves), Damis finds himself in the extraordinary position of the man who is right but cannot prove it. For, after remaining silent in two short scenes, the impostor recoups his position by admitting the truth:

> Oui, mon frère, je suis un méchant, un coupable,
> Un malheureux pécheur, tout plein d'iniquité,
> Le plus grand scélérat qui jamais ait été . . . (1074–6).

There is no denying, after what we have seen, that these words are true; but at the same time they are deceitful. 'They overturn the universal assumptions of language.' Up until now the hypocrite has told lies to conceal the truth; here he tells the truth to conceal the truth. In the 'dépit amoureux' which ended Act II the lovers had spoken falsely of true feelings; here Tartuffe speaks truly of false ones. With a superb confidence, he begs his dupe to consider appearances:

> Non, non: vous vous laissez tromper à l'apparence,
> Je ne suis rien moins, hélas! que ce qu'on pense;
> Tout le monde me prend pour homme de bien;
> Mais la vérité pure est que je ne vaux rien (1097–1100).

With masterful equivocation, Tartuffe pronounces his own conviction in terms hilariously comprehensible to Damis and the spectator, but which convey the opposite to Orgon. Irony can go no farther than to make the truth convey an opposite meaning.

It will not go unnoticed, however, that the truth according to Tartuffe contains even here a notable alloy of prevarication. His sigh ('hélas') is insincere; Tartuffe obviously delights in his hypocritical scheme. Nor does 'tout le monde' take him for an 'homme de bien'. In our experience Tartuffe's admirers are rare and rather foolish. Even this 'confession' contains a misstatement flattering to himself. Tartuffe lies even in telling the truth.

Such also is the effect of his kneeling to pray for Damis' pardon, since pardon implies guilt. But more than in words, this is expressed in action. There is a *crescendo* of movement as Orgon joins Tartuffe on his knees, then in that incongruous position attempts frantically to move from place to place. (It is hardly a scene to stress the dignity of prayer.) There is a sort of farcical *élan* in which the ambush backfires, and at the same time the two kneeling figures offer a beautifully balanced *tableau* to close the act. The mask of Tartuffe has been fixed again in place: 'La volonté du Ciel soit faite en toute chose' (1182). This brilliant line, perhaps the end of the first *Tartuffe*, echoes Orgon's appeal to divine will at the end of Act I and expresses perfectly the churchman's confusion between his own interest and the will of God.

Act IV

The opening scene, which brings the hypocrite together with the 'honnête homme' or man of the world, is a sort of 'gloss' on the previous act. They discuss what we have seen, Cléante thrusting at the weaknesses in Tartuffe's behaviour, the latter deploying all his art to parry the thrust. The comedy lies once more in the ambivalence of his language, which has one meaning for Cléante and quite a different one to the spectator who has actually witnessed Tartuffe's treachery. This device allows Cléante to raise strong objections even to the feigned position of Tartuffe while we laugh at the brazen manner in which he applies a delicate principle falsely to himself. Clearly if it is ever good to accept a gift so that 'tout ce bien ne tombe en de méchantes mains' (1244) this is not a case which proves it, and churchmen who sincerely believed (and believe) in it did not appreciate a scoundrel's using the principle merely for himself. For when the French have once laughed at an idea, they rarely take it seriously afterwards. And what could be more ridiculous than a crook who speaks of keeping stolen property out of evil hands? Or more damaging to the idea than his pretext for breaking off discussion: 'Il est, Monsieur, trois heures et demie' (1266)? Molière's hypocrite shares with other members of the devout party in this play an inclination to silence embarrassing argument. Here Cléante is no more slow to persuade Tartuffe than to persuade Orgon in Act I, but when Tartuffe next breaks off in this manner, it signals his doom.

The hour announced by Tartuffe is also relevant in limiting the time of the action to the twenty-four hours prescribed by the French classic rule of a single day ('unity of time'). Dorine's report that Mariane's marriage has been set 'pour ce soir' (1271) only five lines later shows the crisis is at hand, and it is followed shortly by Orgon with the conventional marriage contract. An animated scene ensues in which Orgon silences argument as effectively as Tartuffe, a relatively crowded stage in comparison with the scenes before and after. Where argument fails, however, Elmire now proposes an ambush which amounts to a controlled experiment upon the piety of Tartuffe:

Je ne vous parle pas de nous ajouter foi;
Mais supposons ici que, d'un lieu qu'on peut prendre,
On vous fît clairement tout voir et tout entendre . . . (1344–6).

Elmire will do by experiment what the logic of Cléante, the mockery of Dorine, and the pleading of Mariane have failed to do: open Orgon's eyes.

But Elmire's is no ordinary experiment. She sends for Tartuffe, so that she is left alone with Orgon, who is persuaded to hide under a table. It is a farcical situation, not unlike that of the husband in Boccaccio's tale of the enchanted pear tree (*Decameron*, IX, 7) adapted by La Fontaine in 1666 (*Contes*, II, 7). In that tale a husband is made to believe that the scene of infidelity in which he actually witnesses his wife from the tree is a mere illusion. But Molière makes Elmire adapt such a situation to undisillusion her husband. She dons a mask in order to remove Tartuffe's (1374–4).

All the themes of *Tartuffe* are again united in this climactic scene in which even Elmire's cough is used ambivalently. Molière now arranges for the 'amour-propre' which had given Tartuffe his hold upon Orgon to upset him. It is no weakness, but in the nature of Molière's conception, that success in the last encounter with Orgon has made Tartuffe as fatuous as his victim, so that after initial wariness he is caught a second time in the same trap. Also if it is instinct or sensuality which exposes Tartuffe's imposture, his self-confidence lowers the guard which had held them in check: 'C'est un homme, entre nous, à mener par le nez' (1524). Elsewhere this might be a simple statement of fact. Molière has Tartuffe state it in circumstances fraught with comic implications: he confides ('entre nous') what Elmire knows perhaps better than he, he is overheard by the man he is confident of duping, he is himself 'led by the nose' by Elmire. Previous surprise, however, has put Tartuffe into a mood to confirm at once the offer of Elmire's heart by what he calls 'des réalités' (1466) and she the 'dernières faveurs' (1458)? The comedy is so constructed that Tartuffe's very concern for experimental proof of her affection results in the success of Elmire's experiment. Both Tartuffe and Elmire want evidence of the other's affection, but for quite different reasons, he for his lust, she to disabuse her husband about his hero and possibly to clear her own reputation. Whatever satire there may be of 'direction of intention' appears to be chiefly designed to carry out Molière's portrait of a rogue.

The comedy here is developed through a masterful use of language, which is at once equivocal and more than ambiguous.

Elmire addresses the same words on different levels to Tartuffe and Orgon, and the poet is confident that they will be understood in still a different way by his audience. Molière realized that 'la plupart des contrariétés viennent d'envelopper dans un même mot des choses opposées'. He might have said of this scene what Corneille had said of his comedy *La Veuve*: 'Le plus beau de leurs entretiens est en équivoques, et en propositions dont ils te laissent les conséquences à tirer . . .' For if Tartuffe is unaware of the comic value of his reassurance: 'Vous êtes assurée ici d'un plein secret' (1503), Elmire has mastered equivocation:

> Mais puisque l'on s'obstine à m'y vouloir réduire,
> Puisqu'on ne veut point croire à tout ce qu'on peut dire,
> Et qu'on veut des témoins qui soient plus convaincants,
> Il faut bien s'y résoudre, et contenter les gens (1513–16).

The genius of the poet lies in the fact that this double reference, immediately intelligible to the audience, escapes Tartuffe and Orgon, who does not emerge until insulted by the unsuspecting Tartuffe. The comedy is heightened by the incongruous *tableau* of the master of the house under a table while his wife is pursued by a guest in semi-ecclesiastical dress.

Then there is an abrupt change of tone of which Molière is a past master and which contributes so strikingly to the rhythm of this play. After a final gesture of farce (Tartuffe walking into Orgon's arms), the act is brought to a close on a note of high dramatic tension. The hypocrite once more reverses the results of his exposure, setting his pious mask more firmly in place than ever and threatening to dispossess Orgon through his title to the latter's property. Orgon thus finds himself in the position to which he had reduced Damis at the close of Act III, wrongly disowned but unable to prove it, and doubly menaced by 'certaine cassette' in Tartuffe's hands.

Act V

The conclusion of *Tartuffe* has been called inferior to the rest of the play despite its high level of suspense and succession of extremely comic scenes. If the intrigue is untidily finished, however, the same may not be said of the act in terms of comic themes. Interpreted in these terms, the last act is the natural fulfilment of those which precede it. Even the 'cassette' which is so suddenly introduced at the end of Act IV is made to represent the 'mental restrictions' which accompanied Orgon's piety under Tartuffe's direction. By turning over a friend's secret to his director, Orgon had prepared denial of possession in such a way that he might 'faire des serments contre la vérité' (1592). Orgon's attack upon the devout also permits Cléante to direct attention to his true character:

Dans la droite raison jamais n'entre la vôtre,
Et toujours d'un excès vous vous jetez dans l'autre (1609–10).

The 'emportement' of the father is then confirmed by the return of Damis, ready to attack Tartuffe and 'lui couper les deux oreilles' (1634). This permits a reflection by Cléante which prepares the *dénouement*:

Nous vivons sous un règne et sommes dans un temps
Où par violence on fait mal ses affaires (1640–1).

Once more the urgency of these scenes is cut short, now by the entrance of Madame Pernelle, Elmire, Mariane and Dorine. There is a full restatement of the credulity theme, a 'juste retour' in the words of Dorine (1695) and doubtless for the spectator. It is an exceedingly comic scene in which Orgon's anxiety turns momentarily to rage with his mother, an irrelevant reaction: 'Nous perdons des moments en bagatelles pures', remarks Cléante (1697). The themes of self-righteousness and credulity are brought together with that of irrelevant behaviour to offer a pure comic image of their futility.

If Madame Pernelle fulfils the credulity theme, M. Loyal now extends the portrait of hypocrisy. The comic aspect of what has been called 'legal truth' can be carried no farther. Thanks to a document in his hands, M. Loyal is to dispossess Orgon in favour of Tartuffe. After Tartuffe's apology for sin in secret, we are asked to look at the falsehood that a paper makes 'true'. There is a comic substitution of the written for the real, the irony of which is reinforced by the ostensible civility of M. Loyal. The comedy in Orgon's desire to force an unwanted marriage upon his daughter and call it her own choice is at last fully focused in this image. There is no more dangerous a man than the one who can remark after a legal, but wrongful, dispossession: 'Le Ciel vous tienne en joie' (1809). He is also deeply comic. But we may laugh only when our attention is diverted from the danger, and this is doubtless why at this moment Madame Pernelle 'tombe des nues' (1814). The evidence has finally convinced her; and as at the beginning of the play it was through her that we were introduced to this extraordinary situation, it is now her 'conversion' that suggests that the spectator might reconsider some of his own opinions.

But just as the last of Tartuffe's admirers is convinced, Valère enters to announce Tartuffe's triumph. Orgon must flee before Tartuffe himself returns to ensure that a royal command for his arrest is executed. There is a mighty *crescendo* of dramatic tension as Tartuffe enters with the Exempt, and Tartuffe is himself arrested. Arguments that this *deus* or rather *rex ex machina* by which Orgon is saved is merely contrived to flatter the King, it seems to me, do not withstand examination of the rhythm and themes of the comedy. Francisque Sarcey reports that audiences respond well to the Exempt. The sudden fall of Tartuffe is a *coup de théâtre*, prepared by Cléante's remarks upon the reign in which they live, but clearly destined to surprise. It fits into a series of comic *revirements* which end Acts III and IV, in which twice a Tartuffe we had thought cornered manages to triumph through imposture. Here, apparently triumphant, he falls.

Let us consider the preparation. Rhythmically, the urgency with which this act opens is relieved by a farcical scene of wrong-headedness and rage. This is followed by a scene which reintroduces dramatic tension in deeply comic circumstances, in turn relieved momentarily by the comic *revirement* of Madame Pernelle. The entries of Valère and Tartuffe successively raise dramatic tension to its highest pitch. The mask theme is then reintroduced (altered now to one of political hypocrisy) and the theme of unanswered reason, for it is Tartuffe himself who precipitates his own arrest by once more breaking off Cléante's reasonable argument. If the logic of events had been twice overthrown outrageously in the preceding acts by Tartuffe's imposture, the play ends with a final 'juste retour' which satisfies aesthetically our hunger for justice. Tartuffe's inhuman scheme has been defeated, and the young people may marry.

3. Style

However unnatural French alexandrines may appear to the English reader today, this highly artificial mode of expression offered no obstacle to early audiences of *Tartuffe*. The public was accustomed to verse as an alternative form of expression to prose and especially to this sonorous verse in twelve syllables, with a caesura or breathing in the middle (though this is varied for special effect), and rhymed in couplets in which masculine and feminine endings alternate. The cadence of verse was one of the ways in which the dramatist heightened reality; and the literate public, schooled equally in the rhetorical laws of verse and prose, must have found verse the natural medium for comedy, though Molière himself and a few of his predecessors also wrote comedies in prose. The preference for verse is perhaps more comprehensible if one realizes that, quite apart from performance, a play (like other literature) was normally read aloud in the seventeenth century; it is not until around this time that we find the first references to non-professionals who read without moving their lips. Farce, of course, when written down at all, was in prose. But for the five-act comedy in the intermediate style, modelled on Plautus and Terence, verse was part of the tradition which Molière continues from Corneille and other distinguished comic poets of the reign of Richelieu and Louis XIII.

The term 'intermediate' denotes a very clear notion of style. In the seventeenth century it had a sort of hierarchical rank comparable in some respects to that of French society itself, then only partially evolved from feudalism. It falls between the ancient concept of the *sermo humilis*, or low style, which was that of popular diction imitated in farce, and the high or 'sublime' style of epic and tragedy. The Alexandrine served also for tragedy and epic, and there it is still more conventional, stylized, even stilted, whereas expression in the intermediate style is modelled (within well-defined rhetorical limits) more nearly upon the living usage of Court and City.

There are indications that Molière once nourished ambitions in the high style; and, had he been more successful as a tragic actor, he might have abandoned, like Corneille, the comic for the tragic muse: it was more distinguished. But Molière's attempt at more elevated diction in the 'comédie héroïque' *Dom Garcie de Navarre* met with little success. Then in *L'Impromptu de Versailles* Molière parodies the emphatic, declamatory way in which Corneille's tragic verse was recited by certain actors. It was probably this very naturalness in recitation which caused the young Racine to withdraw his tragedy *Alexandre* from Molière's troupe in order to give it to a more declamatory group of artists. Written or recited, Molière's diction reflects polite usage, while everything indicates that he was unsuccessful in the high or heroic style and found its more bombastic elements distasteful. His great ambition then in *L'Ecole des Femmes*, in *Tartuffe*, in *Le Misanthrope* and in *Les Femmes Savantes* was to lift comedy in the intermediate style to the dignity of tragedy. This involves the artistic restatement of idiomatic usage which today may seem contrived, but struck his contemporaries above all by its naturalness. 'Enseigne-moi, Molière, où tu trouves la rime', exclaims a contemporary in admiration of the apparent ease of his versification.

Yet if Molière had confined himself exclusively to the intermediate style, *Tartuffe* would scarcely have the stylistic tension which has kept it almost continually before the public for nearly three centuries. Everywhere Molière transcends the style in which he is working. His characters do not all speak alike, and they do not always speak upon the same level. Stylistic variation is used to express difference of character and change of mood. The deep roots of *Tartuffe* in farce already mentioned in other connections are particularly evident in its language. Boileau, whose admiration for the naturalness of Molière's verse was just quoted, later complains that he has 'sans honte à Térence allié Tabarin', or mixed with the intermediate style the techniques of a celebrated juggler who in Molière's youth amused popular audiences at the Pont-Neuf. Boileau is thinking of certain later farces, but what he writes applies also to the admixture of the gesture and speech of farce in *Tartuffe* in violation of the 'unity of tone'. Also it is in just what Boileau disparages, the interplay of the instinctive and the improper with the conventional, the low with the intermediate style, that we find the peculiar triumph of Molière. The deep and exceedingly comic significance of Molière's lapses from the intermediate style escaped Boileau through its very originality.

Obviously it is Dorine who best illustrates this point. As the stage directions note: 'C'est une servante qui parle'; and neither the verse which follows this comment: 'Et s'il vient à roter, il lui dit: "Dieu vous aide!"' (194), nor a remark such as: 'Oui, c'est un beau museau' (560), might be easily distinguished from the low style of farce were it even in prose.

Tartuffe on the other hand trespasses upon the 'sublime'. There is little from a purely stylistic point of view to distinguish his first declaration to Elmire from contemporary tragedy. At least in isolation one might be tempted to attribute the following couplets to Racine or Quinault rather than Molière:

Et je vais être enfin, par votre seul arrêt,
Heureux, si vous voulez, malheureux, s'il vous plaît (959–60),

or (despite a nuance of piety and *préciosité* in this consecrated military image which verges on parody):

> De vos regards divins l'ineffable douceur
> Força la résistance où s'obstinait mon cœur (975–6).

The verbal mask of Tartuffe is one of dignity, and its elevated diction is often near that of tragedy.

Granted that these examples are particularly favourable to this thesis, this comparison of the speech of Dorine and Tartuffe already suggests something of the way in which Molière differentiates his characters stylistically. It should not be forgotten that, limited stage directions aside, almost all we really know about most of them is what they say and do themselves, and what is said about them. The dramatist has nothing of the freedom of the novelist to intervene with his own commentary, or at least this is a freedom which in the seventeenth century was used with discretion in the convention of the 'raisonneur'. What each character himself says remains our best clue to his nature. For example, what Dorine has to say about the reaction of Orgon to Tartuffe's belch offers information about both of those characters, but above all such striking evidence of her own social class that Molière felt obliged to disarm criticism by reminding us that it is after all 'une servante qui parle'. Her words at once place her socially in a popular comic type and, by giving voice to the socially unsayable, suggest the irrepressibility of her temperament which appears also to represent that of human nature itself.

Already we are far beyond the reservations of Boileau, and if now we compare Dorine's style with Cléante's this interpretation is strikingly confirmed. Both argue from a common-sense point of view, but there is a world of difference in their way of reasoning. Examination of almost any of Cléante's speeches would suggest conclusions similar to analysis of this fragment of his expostulation with Orgon in Act I:

Il est de faux dévots ainsi que de faux braves;
Et comme on ne voit pas qu'où l'honneur les conduit
Les vrais braves soient ceux qui font beaucoup de bruit,
Les bons et vrais dévots, qu'on doit suivre à la trace,
Ne sont pas ceux aussi qui font tant de grimace.
Hé quoi? vous ne ferez nulle distinction
Entre l'hypocrisie et la dévotion?
Vous les voulez traiter d'un semblable langage,
Et rendre même honneur au masque qu'au visage,
Egaler l'artifice à la sincérité,
Confondre l'apparence avec la vérité,
Estimer le fantôme autant que la personne,
Et la fausse monnaie à l'égal de la bonne? (326–38).

Indeed this passage is if anything less abstract than the usual language of Cléante, whose expression depends largely upon the abstractions which are one of the great debts of the seventeenth century to Scholasticism. There is nothing concrete about the repeated opposition of concepts like: 'Hypocrisie' *vs.* 'dévotion'; 'artifice' *vs.* 'sincérité'; 'apparence' *vs.* 'vérité'. Such speech springs rather from a long tradition of rationalism which was the handmaiden of theology before it was the harbinger of modern science. It reflects in Cléante a philosophic 'forma mentis' and associates him with the admirers of Descartes, who for many minds dominated his age. There are also images to be sure, but they are literary and conventional, consecrated by use: 'faux braves', 'à la trace', 'masque', 'fantôme', 'fausse monnaie'. The image of counterfeiters in devotion is perhaps as near as Molière ever comes to a formative or poetically creative use of language in *Tartuffe*, with the sole exception of Dorine's famous neologism 'tartuffiée' (674). Elsewhere we look in vain for that re-creation of language which Shakespeare (or the Elizabethans?) may have led us to expect in a great dramatic poet.

Now Dorine also is familiar with rational arguments At times she reasons with the same abstract logic as Cléante:

Qui d'une sainte vie embrasse l'innocence
Ne doit point tant prôner son nom et sa naissance,

Et l'humble procédé de la dévotion
Souffre mal les éclats de cette ambition (497–500).

To attribute these verses to Dorine at first sight one would need to know this play extremely well. Indeed we know from the *Lettre sur l'Imposteur* that in an earlier version of *Tartuffe* these or similar verses were addressed to Orgon by Cléante. As Dorine's speech progresses, however, it is unmistakably identified as her own by very pointed allusions to 'cocuage'. Behind the rational in this servant always lurks the unmentionable, and it falls to Dorine to express what Cléante passes in silence. In a very real sense it is through the comic expression of what politeness banned that Molière was the 'liberator of his age'.

It is not then 'out of character', as sometimes argued, for Dorine to begin speeches in the upper levels of the intermediate style. All we know of her character is what is in the text, and the fact is that she often so begins an argument. But she cannot or will not (does not) complete it upon the same level. As the rational argument is developed in the intermediate style, the pressure of naked fact builds up behind it until the outrageous, but unmentionable, circumstances which necessarily belong to the low style seem to explode into words. It is the deepest meaning of Molière that the mask of convention is torn away. A device repugnant to Boileau is used to probe the ultimate reaches of comedy.

Let us examine Molière's technique. Cléante might have recommended to Mariane the following reply to Orgon:

Lui dire qu'un cœur n'aime point par autrui,
Que vous vous mariez pour vous, non pas pour lui,
Qu'étant celle pour qui se fait toute l'affaire,
C'est à vous, non à lui, que le mari doit plaire . . . (591–4).

That is sensible advice, unexceptionably expressed in the intermediate style. It has been suggested, however, that opponents to such advice were probably as numerous in the first audiences as sympathizers; and it is doubtful that even such a clear statement of the issue as this would have provoked much laughter. It is the concluding sally which at once distinguishes Dorine from Cléante and offers a poetic counterpart of Orgon's outrageous behaviour:

> Et si son Tartuffe est pour lui si charmant,
> Il le peut épouser sans nul empêchement (595–6).

Molière's genius is in this nonsense that goes deeper than sense. For the very element in Dorine's conclusion which defies reason offers a comic image of Orgon's attitude. This is art that transcends argument. It is the logical, the illogical, the verbal correlative of Orgon's deeply comic egoism.

This is no isolated phenomenon. A similar process may be observed in Dorine's reply to Tartuffe's order to cover her bosom when he first appears on stage:

> Vous êtes donc bien tendre à la tentation,
> Et la chair sur vos sens fait grande impression?
> Certes je ne sais quelle chaleur vous monte:
> Mais à convoiter, moi, je ne suis point si prompte,
> Et je vous verrais nu du haut jusques en bas,
> Que toute votre peau ne me tenterait pas (863–8).

The first couplet is brusque. It picks up Tartuffe in his own language: 'tendre', 'tentation', 'chair', 'sens', 'impression'. In 'chaleur' and 'convoiter' of the following couplet, however, the inhuman in Tartuffe's pose is confronted with the animal facts of life by a delightful mixture of the vocabulary of theology with that of animal husbandry. Then in the last couplet Dorine touches upon the idea which is as comically abhorrent to the 'faux dévot' as to Molière's 'précieuses ridicules': that of 'un homme vraiment nu'. Dorine's disparaging allusion to the naked man is outrageous to contemporary 'bienséance', but it points up the comic illusions of Tartuffe, whether as lustful man or ascetic mask. For there is a special, doubtless very cruel, irony in the fact that all of his skin is tempted, but not tempting. This lapse of tone foreshadows alike the instinct and the inability which undo him, the unmasking which results not from his attempt, but his failure, to seduce Elmire. This man is mocked on every level. It is his punishment, as Arthur Rimbaud appreciated, to be stripped in this play 'nu du haut jusques en bas'.

Comparison with this sally of a verse each of Tartuffe himself and Orgon is instructive. Its deep meaning is very nearly the same as that of Orgon's inarticulate effort at praising Tartuffe in Act I: 'C'est un homme . . . qui . . . ha! . . . un homme . . . un homme enfin' (272), which inadvertently goes beneath Tartuffe's mask to express the fact that he is first of all a man, but not one about whom much can be found to praise, and in fact (his inhuman 'piety' notwithstanding) only a man. With this we may compare again what Tartuffe confesses to Elmire: 'Ah! pour être dévot, je n'en suis pas moins homme' (966). The unctuous Tartuffe restates in the high style of his imposture (this line in fact is taken from Corneille's tragedy *Sertorius* with the stylistically negligible substitution of 'dévot' for 'Romain') the inarticulate muttering of Orgon and the crude sally of Dorine. Once again more is said than meant. What is said in each case points to the same thing. How it is said betrays the speaker.

The devices of repetition ('Et Tartuffe?') and equivocation have been discussed in connection with structure and require no general analysis here. Still it should be kept in mind that the verse of dramatic poetry serves not only to delineate characters and get them from event to event, but also to move them physically from place to place on stage. This is particularly important in a comedy like *Tartuffe* where there is a great deal of stage action. Actors have noticed that often what might be taken for padding in a verse actually performs the useful function of allowing the speaker sufficient time for some significant movement or gesture. A clumsy construction may also, as we have just seen, reflect inarticulate thought. It frequently renders a temporary state of surprise or agitation.

Mariane's reply to Orgon's embarrassed demand to declare herself for Tartuffe in Act II is a case in point:

Qui voulez-vous, mon père, que je dise
Qui me touche le cœur, et qu'il me serait doux
De voir par votre choix devenir mon époux? (446–8).

This is a comic repetition of Orgon's own tortuous exposition of a devious plan, and like Orgon she withholds the key word 'époux' until the last possible moment. Repetition of this clumsy construction in the doubly awkward interrogative form expresses at once the surprise and instinctive disbelief of Mariane, and the unstraightforward conduct of her father. Here again in Molière's style may be found a verbal equivalent to Orgon's action. It is only for the purpose of study that Molière's style may be divorced from his meaning.

Clearly in such passages Molière obtains his comic effect through a process which is just the reverse of the polished wit of Restoration comedy or, to take a nearer example, Oscar Wilde. Molière's company often played a great French comedy of wit, *Les Visionnaires* of Desmarets de Saint-Sorlin, but Molière continues its intellectual themes of obsession and self-deception rather than its style. It is characteristic that for his supreme achievement in *Tartuffe* Molière often employs a style which, paradoxically, is distinguished above all by its clumsiness. Let us examine the last long speech of Elmire in that climactic scene of Act IV in which Tartuffe presses his seduction while Orgon refuses to intervene:

Enfin je vois qu'il faut se résoudre à céder,
Qu'il faut que je consente à vous tout accorder,
Et qu'à moins de cela je ne dois point prétendre
Qu'on puisse être content, et qu'on veuille se rendre.
Sans doute il est fâcheux d'en venir jusque-là,
Et c'est bien malgré moi que je franchis cela;
Mais puisque l'on s'obstine à m'y vouloir réduire,
Puisqu'on ne veut point croire à tout ce qu'on peut dire,
Et qu'on veut des témoins qui soient plus convaincants,
Il faut s'y bien résoudre, et contenter les gens (1507–16).

There is no need to insist again upon the masterful ambiguity of this passage and the appropriateness of its placing. From a narrow stylistic point of view, however, it is obvious that out of context this verse must seem padded and mediocre. There is nothing independently witty or memorable here. There are no *sententiae* to take away.

Yet it is Elmire who voices perhaps the most important one of the play:

> Non: on est aisément dupé par ce qu'on aime,
> Et l'amour-propre engage à se tromper soi-même (1357–8).

And as Elmire sums up the wisdom of the play, Tartuffe has just epitomized its wickedness:

> Le scandale du monde est ce qui fait l'offense,
> Et ce n'est pas pécher que pécher en silence (1505–6).

Clearly if Elmire does not then continue in such round and well-wrought verse, it is because the poet's interest is elsewhere. For these verses express many things through amplification and ambiguity. To begin with, we do not really progress on the first level of meaning from the necessity of resolve which Elmire announces in v. 1507 to its repetition in v. 1516. We turn in a circle where ten verses are required to express what might have been stated in two. Molière dramatizes the fact that Elmire is nearing the end of her resources.

The complicated succession of 'que' clauses in the first of these two sentences (there are five of them in four verses) marks the successive stages of Elmire's retreat and allows her time—physically—for strategic withdrawal. Then finally in v. 1510 she finds a formula capable of putting off Tartuffe while appealing to Orgon in the same words. In the second sentence concessive and causal subordinates are piled up to voice Elmire's mounting exasperation. Tartuffe sees meaning in words almost devoid of meaning upon that level, while Orgon fails to respond to their concealed urgency. Dramatic tension is built up in this speech by the importunity of Tartuffe and the inaction of Orgon. Its comic force is for the spectator in its complicated clarity.

It may be argued that Molière's stylistic achievement, here and elsewhere, is not in the very front rank of literary artistry; and if the front rank is limited to poets like Shakespeare and Dante the argument would almost certainly be convincing. Molière shares the general weakness of his age and country in visual imagery. Images such as 'éclat' and 'flamme' were already well worn when they reached Molière, and their use is intellectual rather than perceptive: they no longer represent ideas concretely. Molière's vocabulary leans heavily towards words with an ethical rather than visual background. It would hardly be in the style of Molière to write of 'Vaulting ambition, which o'erleaps itself | And falls on th' other side' (*Macbeth*). When Dorine mentions ambition, it is to oppose it to '. . . l'humble procédé de la dévotion' (499). Ambition is not giv en an 'objective correlative', it is simply judged. Though doubtless exceptions may be found, the following alexandrine of Damis may represent many others: 'L'injurieux aveu d'une coupable flamme' (1062). It is highly successful in its way, a 'vers nombreux' in which a long adjective followed by a short noun in the first hemistich is deliberately balanced by a similar construction in the second (*cf.* 1000). But clearly 'flamme' (love) has no more *visual* force than 'aveu'; and if it had, the balance of the verse would be broken. The two adjectives, moreover, are strictly ethical qualifications. That is perhaps to be expected in this accusation; but throughout *Tartuffe* there is a marked preference for ethical assessment which obtains generally in this author and period of French literature. The whole aim of the poet stylistically seems to be in balanced expression of this moral judgement by Damis upon the sentiment and confession of Tartuffe.

Against this Alexandrine may be set another verse from *Macbeth* which states an ethical concept concretely: 'But screw your courage to the sticking place . . .', admonishes Lady Macbeth. There is no concern here for either ethical judgement or its balanced statement. Everything is in the image. It is a 'unification of disparate ideas'. It builds its idea upon an object. Molière's method is very different. He belongs to a great tradition of moralists and rhetoricians whose stylistic aim was to intervene, setting forth reality in terms of ideas, hardly ever to find correlatives for the latter. But he belongs also to a tradition of comic actors in which the comic image is seldom conveyed solely by language, but by the situation, timing, and tone in which it is used.

What Molière is not must not then obscure what he is. Such comparison is useful only in so far as it focuses attention upon an author's own achievement. For we are as little likely to settle the debate upon the relative merits of French Classicism and the Elizabethans as the more ancient one between tragedy and comedy. Each work in the last analysis must be interpreted in its own terms, and in style as in structure Molière's achievement here is very great. From start to end his play is filled with comic language, comic attitudes, gestures and ambiguity which on his own stage would and could leave no doubt. Molière is the master of comic ambivalence. In *Tartuffe* also he has reconciled the severe restrictions of a literary convention with the situations of farce to create characters now a part of the French language. That is a summit of literary achievement. No one has yet appeared, in France or elsewhere, who could challenge Molière's comic vision, his mastery of that 'contrariété' of character betrayed when words are made to convey a hidden meaning. Other poets excel in visual imagery. With no such resources, Molière has found comic images of unrivalled mastery.

Select Bibliography

EDITIONS

Oeuvres de Molière—ed. Despois and Mesnard (Grands Ecrivains de la France). Paris, 1873–93. Vol. IV.

Théâtre Complet—ed. R. Jouanny. Paris, Garnier, 1960. 2 vols.

Le Tartuffe, ed. Pierre Clarac, Classiques Larousse.

Le Tartuffe . . ., mise en scene . . . de Fernand Ledoux. Paris, 1953. (Suggestive remarks on the staging of *Tartuffe*.)

ON MOLIÈRE

Adam, Antoine, *Histoire de la littérature française au XVIIe siècle*. Paris, 1948–56. Vol. III: *L'Apogée du siècle: Boileau, Molière*.

Descotes, Maurice, *Les grands rôles du théâtre de Molière*, Paris, 1960.

Fernandez, Ramon, *La Vie de Molière*. Paris, 1930. (A stimulating biographical reconstruction, also available in translation: *Molière: The Man Seen Through His Plays*. New York, 1958. Also article 'Molière' in *Tableau de la littérature française, XVIIe et XVIIIe siècles*, ed. André Gide. Paris, 1939.

Lancaster, H. C., *A History of French Dramatic Literature in the Seventeenth Century*. Baltimore, 1929–42. Part III: *The Period of Molière*.

Michaut, G., *La Jeunesse de Molière, Les Débuts de Molière à Paris, Les Luttes de Molière*, Paris. 1922–25.

Moore, W. G., *Molière, A New Criticism*. Oxford, 1949.

Mornet, Daniel, *Molière*. Paris, 1943.

Simon, Alfred, *Molière par lui-même*. Paris, 1957.

ON 'TARTUFFE'

Auerbach, Erich, 'The *Faux Dévot*', in *Mimesis*, tr. W. Trask. Princeton, 1953.

Baumal, F., *Tartuffe et ses avatars*. Paris, 1925.

Cairncross, John, *New Light on Molière*. Geneva, 1956.

Emard, P., *Tartuffe, sa vie et son milieu et la comédie de Molière*. Paris, 1932.

Moore, W. G., '*Tartuffe* and the comic principle', in *Modern Language Review*, Jan., 1948.

A Bibliographical Note for the 1976 Impression

Publications commemorating the tercentenary of Molière's death are too numerous to summarize here, and few are more relevant than those mentioned in the Bibliographical Note for the 1965 impression as follows:

Three important recent critical studies of Molière contain sections on *Tartuffe*: J. D. Hubert, *Molière and the Comedy of the Intellect*, University of California Press, 1962; L. Gossman, *Men and Masks, A Study of Molière*, Johns Hopkins University Press, 1963; and J. Guicharnaud, *Molière, une aventure théâtrale*, Paris, Gallimard, 1963. Professor Guicharnaud has also edited a useful volume in the series 'Twentieth Century Views', *Molière, a Collection of Critical Essays*, Englewood Cliffs, N.J., Prentice-Hall, 1964. Briefly, his interpretation suggests that Orgon's household symbolizes on one level a monarchy under the influence of an evil counsellor, contrasted in the *dénouement* with the France of Louis XIV; and he argues that if Molière's anti-social characters (Tartuffe, Orgon) are eventually disarmed, they are not converted, a dramatic structure said to reflect a pessimistic view of human nature. But in '*Tartuffe*, Religion and Courtly Culture', E. S. Chill advances the interesting hypothesis that in *Tartuffe* 'political obedience is linked to an optimistic view of the human passions' to which Orgon is rallied in the *dénouement* (*French Historical Studies*, III, 2, 1963). A. J. Guibert, *Bibliographie des Œuvres de Molière publiées au XVIIe siècle*, Paris, Centre National de la Recherche Scientifique, 1961, 2 vols., makes an important contribution to Molière textual criticism. M. Jurgens and E. Maxfield-Miller, *Cent Ans de recherches sur Molière*, Paris, Imprimerie Nationale, 1963, is a valuable collection of carefully analysed Molière documents, many previously unpublished. H. P. Salomon, *Tartuffe devant l'opinion française*, Paris, Presses universitaires, 1962, studies the fortune of the play in France and in French Canada. I should like to add that the best edition of Molière is now the *Œuvres Complètes*, ed. G. Couton, 2 vols., Bibliothèque de la Pléiade, 1971. J. Schérer, *Structures de Tartuffe*, Paris, SEDES, 1966, deserves mention, as do the following general studies: S. Chevalley, *Molière en son temps*, Geneva, Minkoff, 1973 (beautifully illustrated); A. Eustis, *Molière as Ironic Contemplator*, The Hague, Mouton, 1973; R. Jasinski, *Molière*, Paris, Hatier, 1969; and W. D. Howarth and M. Thomas, *Molière: Stage and Study*, Oxford University Press, 1973 (essays in honour of W. G. Moore). I discuss 'The present state of Molière studies' (to mid 1972) in another collection of essays, *Molière and the Commonwealth of Letters*, College and University Press of Mississippi, 1975, and reconsider 'Some background to Molière's *Tartuffe*' in *Australian Journal of French Studies* X, 2, 1973.